U.S. Air Force Enlisted Classification and Reclassification

Potential Improvements Using Machine Learning and Optimization Models

SEAN ROBSON, MARIA C. LYTELL, MATTHEW WALSH,
KIMBERLY CURRY HALL, KIRSTEN M. KELLER, VIKRAM KILAMBI,
JOSHUA SNOKE, JONATHAN W. WELBURN, PATRICK S. ROBERTS,
OWEN HALL, LOUIS T. MARIANO

Prepared for the Department of the Air Force
Approved for public release; distribution unlimited

RAND PROJECT AIR FORCE

For more information on this publication, visit **www.rand.org/t/RRA284-1**.

About RAND

The RAND Corporation is a research organization that develops solutions to public policy challenges to help make communities throughout the world safer and more secure, healthier and more prosperous. RAND is nonprofit, nonpartisan, and committed to the public interest. To learn more about RAND, visit www.rand.org.

Research Integrity

Our mission to help improve policy and decisionmaking through research and analysis is enabled through our core values of quality and objectivity and our unwavering commitment to the highest level of integrity and ethical behavior. To help ensure our research and analysis are rigorous, objective, and nonpartisan, we subject our research publications to a robust and exacting quality-assurance process; avoid both the appearance and reality of financial and other conflicts of interest through staff training, project screening, and a policy of mandatory disclosure; and pursue transparency in our research engagements through our commitment to the open publication of our research findings and recommendations, disclosure of the source of funding of published research, and policies to ensure intellectual independence. For more information, visit www.rand.org/about/principles.

RAND's publications do not necessarily reflect the opinions of its research clients and sponsors.

Library of Congress Cataloging-in-Publication Data is available for this publication.

ISBN: 978-1-9774-0702-3

Cover: photo by Senior Airman Levin Boland/U.S. Air Force.

Preface

Recent trends in initial skills training (IST) indicate that the number of U.S. Air Force (USAF) enlisted personnel reclassified into other occupational specialties has increased in recent years, with a steady rise having occurred between fiscal years 2013 and 2017. Career field reclassification can result in a wide range of negative outcomes, including increased costs, delayed manning, training schedule challenges, and decreased morale. Career field reclassification cannot be addressed without understanding the broader context of career field classification. To understand and address the challenge of IST reclassification, Headquarters Air Education and Training Command expressed interest in exploring options for improving processes to classify and reclassify enlisted active-duty, non–prior service airmen for IST. In this report we outline key findings from a 2019 study that employed qualitative and quantitative analyses, including machine learning (ML) models, to assess predictors of IST success (and failure), as well as testing of an optimization model to identify opportunities for improving reclassification decisions. We conclude with recommendations on ways for the USAF to realize the full potential of contemporary ML tools to increase the quality of classification and reclassification decisions.

The work reported here should be of interest to military policymakers and researchers involved in setting and evaluating military classification and reclassification processes. The work in this report was sponsored by the Director of Operations and Communications, Headquarters Air Education and Training Command, USAF. This project was conducted within the Workforce, Development, and Health Program of RAND Project AIR FORCE (PAF).

RAND Project AIR FORCE

RAND PAF, a division of the RAND Corporation, is the Department of the Air Force's (DAF's) federally funded research and development center for studies and analyses. PAF provides the DAF with independent analyses of policy alternatives affecting the development, employment, combat readiness, and support of current and future air, space, and cyber forces. Research is conducted in four programs: Strategy and Doctrine; Force Modernization and Employment; Resource Management; and Workforce, Development, and Health. The research reported here was prepared under contract FA7014-16-D-1000.

Additional information about PAF is available on our website:
www.rand.org/paf/

This report documents work originally shared with the DAF on September 12, 2019. The draft report, issued on September 30, 2019, was reviewed by formal peer reviewers and DAF subject-matter experts.

Contents

Figures

Tables

Summary

Issue

Every year, thousands of people enlist in the U.S. Air Force (USAF) and are classified into hundreds of occupational specialties.[1] Although most airmen successfully complete initial skills training (IST), about 10 percent are eliminated. Eliminated airmen are either separated from USAF or reclassified into other specialties. Given recent increases in reclassification, we set out to identify what could affect IST success and to determine if classification and reclassification processes can be improved.

Approach

The study team employed a mixed methods approach that included: (1) review of USAF and Department of Defense (DoD) policies, and relevant academic and policy research literature; (2) interviews with subject-matter experts (SMEs) on enlisted classification and reclassification processes; (3) focus groups with airmen in select specialties; (4) analyses employing traditional statistical models and machine learning (ML) approaches; and (5) development of a linear integer (optimization) model for reclassification that considers both airmen mission readiness outcomes and cost.

Conclusions

- Increasing the number of relevant predictor variables can increase the accuracy of ML predictions. Expanding the set of predictor variables generally decreased prediction errors by approximately 5 percent.
- Occupational classification is designed to optimize training success but not other important outcomes. ML models may be most useful in identifying optimal specialty assignments to improve other career outcomes such as early separation and reenlistment.
- Reclassification is a manual process and can be optimized to achieve slightly better training and career outcomes while also reducing current costs.
- Focus groups identified gaps in USAF information about airmen characteristics, training environment, and job activities. Addressing issues identified in the focus groups could help to reduce training eliminations.

---

[1] This report was completed before the creation of the U.S. Space Force and therefore uses the name "U.S. Air Force" to refer to both the air and space services.

Recommendations

Based on our analyses, we identified specific recommendations focused on data and data quality, selection and classification processes, and the training environment. Many of these recommendations can be adopted now to improve the current USAF classification and reclassification system, whether or not ML is implemented (see Table S.1).

Table S.1. Recommendations for Improving Enlisted Classification and Reclassification

1. Expand the set of predictors and outcomes used in USAF enlisted classifications.

Predictors such as the following can be used to improve matches between airmen and specialties and, in turn, career outcomes:

- Archive Technical Training Management System–Job Match and other relevant data used to qualify airmen for USAF specialties (AFSs)
- Require all recruits to complete the USAF-Work Interest Navigator (AF-WIN), a vocational interests inventory, and recruiters to educate recruits on the specialties tied to AF-WIN results
- Systematically collect information about job requirements
- Develop a structured biodata instrument that is completed by all recruits
- Consider using peers and IST instructors to rate personality.

Outcomes such as the following listed can be used to measure individual airman performance and career outcomes:

- Define and systematically measure outcomes beyond those associated with IST success (e.g., job satisfaction, organizational citizenship behaviors, counterproductive work behaviors)
- Systematically examine impact of training environment on airmen's training success
- Monitor the moving averages for graduation rate by specialty.

2. Improve data quality, comprehensiveness, and access to develop and implement ML models.

- Use a data quality framework for selection and classification variables
- Establish data stewards or custodian(s) to oversee data quality.

3. Update classification processes to improve job-match outcomes so that airmen not only succeed in training but also perform well on the job.

- Replace Job Spin inputs with probabilities for different outcomes
- Consider integrating reclassification decisions into Job Spin
- Consider expanding the time horizon for assigning reclassified airmen.

4. Address common ML challenges prior to implementation, including ethics and privacy, interpretability of ML models, and model performance.

The value of contemporary modeling has been demonstrated for many organizational functions, including personnel management. USAF collects and stores data on individuals, such as those listed in the predictors box in Figure S.1, as part of its personnel management processes. These data can be used as inputs to analytical modeling methods to improve selection and assignment of individuals to jobs to improve outcomes, such as training success, job performance, and retention.

Figure S.1. Analytical Linkages Between Predictors and Outcomes

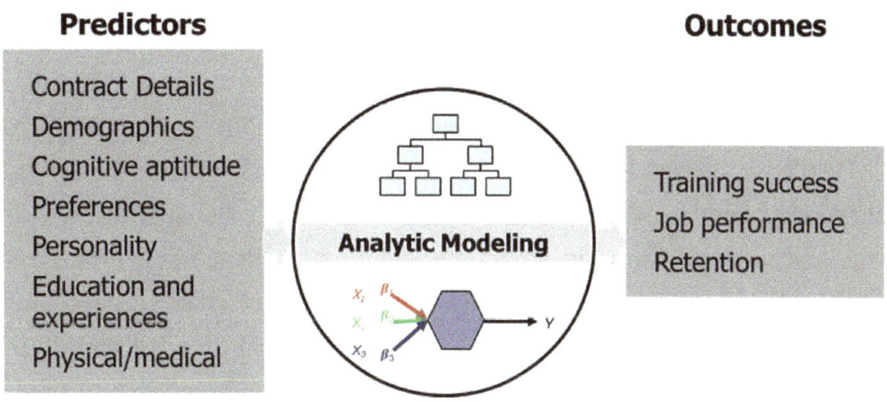

Acknowledgments

Many people made this project a success. We begin by thanking our sponsor, Brig Gen William Spangenthal. We also express gratitude to our action officer, Lt Col Steven Dillenburger, who assisted our efforts.

Several individuals throughout the USAF deserve our gratitude. We appreciate the expertise, data support, and guidance from Ken Schwartz and the team at Air Force Personnel Center (AFPC)/Strategic Research and Assessment Branch (DSYX) including Laura Barron, Johnny Weissmuller, Mark Rose, James Johnson, and John Trent. We also thank those from Second Air Force including Andy Donate, Doug Mettler, and several other key staff for providing content knowledge, data, and feedback on training and reclassification processes. Finally, we are grateful to several other USAF offices and personnel including those who oversee personnel systems (e.g., Technical Training Management System [TTMS] and Air Force Recruiting Information Support System [AFRISS]) for helping provide access to data and responding to inquiries about possible sources of data.

We also extend our gratitude to the airmen who took time out of their day to participate in our focus groups and to the experts who participated in our policy discussions. We learned valuable information about the opportunities and challenges of classification, reclassification, and training from the focus group and interview participants. We also thank the career field and training management staff for their support for the project, including helping with logistics at the training locations where we held focus groups.

We also thank several of our RAND colleagues. Ray Conley, former Director of the RAND PAF Manpower, Personnel, and Training Program, provided guidance and support throughout the project. Bart Bennett and John Crown offered their guidance on USAF policy and modeling to our analysts. Paul Emslie and Anthony Lawrence procured personnel data, answered the team's data-related questions, and provided programming services. Nathan Vest and Mary Kate Adgie were critical to the success of our focus groups: They took and cleaned notes, entered data, and assisted with initial coding. We also received support on focus group activities from Isabel Leamon, Norah Griffin, and David Catt (note-taking) and Sarah Weilant (facilitating discussions). Barbara Bicksler edited and streamlined our report and summary. Matthew Strawn reviewed and summarized personnel selection literature. Finally, Christina Dozier scheduled project travel and assisted with document formatting.

Abbreviations

2AF	Second Air Force
2AF/Det 1	Second Air Force, Detachment 1
AAE	Active Enlisted Personnel Extracts
ADSS	AETC Decision Support System
AETC	Air Education and Training Command
AFPC	Air Force Personnel Center
AFQT	Armed Forces Qualification Test
AFS	Air Force specialty
AFRISS	Air Force Recruiting Information Support System
AFRISS-TF	Air Force Recruiting Information Support System—Total Force
AFSC	Air Force specialty code
AF-WIN	Air Force Work Interest Navigator
ASVAB	Armed Services Vocational Aptitude Battery
ATC	air traffic control
ATC-ST	Air Traffic Control Scenario Test
AUC	area under the curve
BART	Bayesian additive regression tree
BMT	basic military training
CART	classification and regression tree
CEA	Career Enlisted Aviation
DEP	Delayed Entry Program
DLAB	Defense Language Aptitude Battery
DoD	Department of Defense
DSYX	Strategic Research and Assessment Branch
EDPT	Electronic Data Processing Test

EIS	Enlisted Initial Skills
EMT	emergency medical technician
EP	electronic protection
EPR	Enlisted Performance Report
EW	electronic warfare
FY	Fiscal year
GAA	Guaranteed Aptitude Area
GLM	general linear model
GTEP	Guaranteed Training Enlistment Program
HRM	human resource management
IST	initial skills training
IT	information technology
JROTC	Junior Reserve Officers' Training Corps
MAGE	mechanical aptitude, administrative aptitude, general aptitude, electronic aptitude
MEPS	Military Entrance Processing Station
MilPDS	Military Personnel Data System
ML	machine learning
MTI	military training instructor
MTL	military training leader
NN	neural network
NPS	non–prior service
PAF	Project AIR FORCE
PGL	Program Guidance Letter
PT	physical training
PULHES	physical condition, upper extremities, lower extremities, hearing, vision, and psychiatric stability
RF	random forest
ROC	receiver operator characteristic

SAT	Strength Aptitude Test
SME	subject-matter expert
SVM	support vector machine
TAPAS	Tailored Adaptive Personality Assessment System
TOE	term of enlistment
TTMS	Technical Training Management System
TTMS-JM	Technical Training Management System–Job Match
USAF	U.S. Air Force

1. Introduction and Background

Every year, thousands of people enlist in the U.S. Air Force (USAF) and are sorted into hundreds of enlisted occupational specialties.[1] To complete this sorting—or classification—USAF engages in a range of activities that begin at recruiting and extend through basic military training (BMT). These activities, bolstered by policies and programs, comprise USAF enlisted classification system, which has the purpose of ensuring that airmen with particular qualifications, aptitudes, and attributes are assigned to appropriate enlisted occupational specialties in the right proportions to execute USAF missions.[2]

However, not all USAF enlisted personnel successfully complete the initial skills training (IST) for their occupational specialties, known as USAF specialties (AFSs).[3] Some of these airmen are removed (i.e., eliminated) from IST and leave USAF. Many others stay in USAF but are sent to IST for other AFSs. Airmen who are eliminated from one AFS and sent to another are termed *reclassifications*.

Reclassifications come with costs. USAF expends resources to make decisions on where to send these airmen and then to move them to other training locations. Additional costs are associated with time spent training in an AFS from which airmen were eliminated and for which they are retrained. In fiscal year (FY) 2018, the costs associated with training time for airmen who were reclassified totaled approximately $68 million.[4] Reclassifications also create logistical challenges for training schedules and have longer-term effects of delaying manning in AFSs where there have been losses, which may affect morale in those AFSs.

USAF experienced a surge in the number of reclassifications in recent years. Figure 1.1 shows reclassifications from FY 2006–2018. Spikes in reclassifications occurred in 2009 and 2017, with a steady rise occurring between FY 2013–2017. The dashed line represents the average number of reclassifications (~1,660) across the years represented in the figure.

Although the number of reclassifications fluctuates over time, the *rates* of reclassification have not fluctuated as dramatically, as showing in Figure 1.2.

---

[1] This report was completed before the creation of the U.S. Space Force and therefore uses the name "U.S. Air Force" to refer to both the air and space services.

[2] U.S. Air Force Recruiting Service Instruction 36-2001, "Recruiting Procedure for the Air Force," 2012.

[3] AFSs are occupations with associated duties, tasks, and positions that require airmen to have specific sets of knowledge, skills, abilities, and other attributes. USAF clusters AFSs into career fields that align with broad functional and mission areas (aircrew operations, aircraft maintenance, intelligence, cyber, medical, and so on).

[4] Estimated using FY 2015 USAF specialty-specific technical training costs provided by USAF. FY 2015 is the last time the cost model was updated.

Figure 1.1. Number of Airmen Reclassified in Initial Skills Training, Fiscal Years 2006–2018

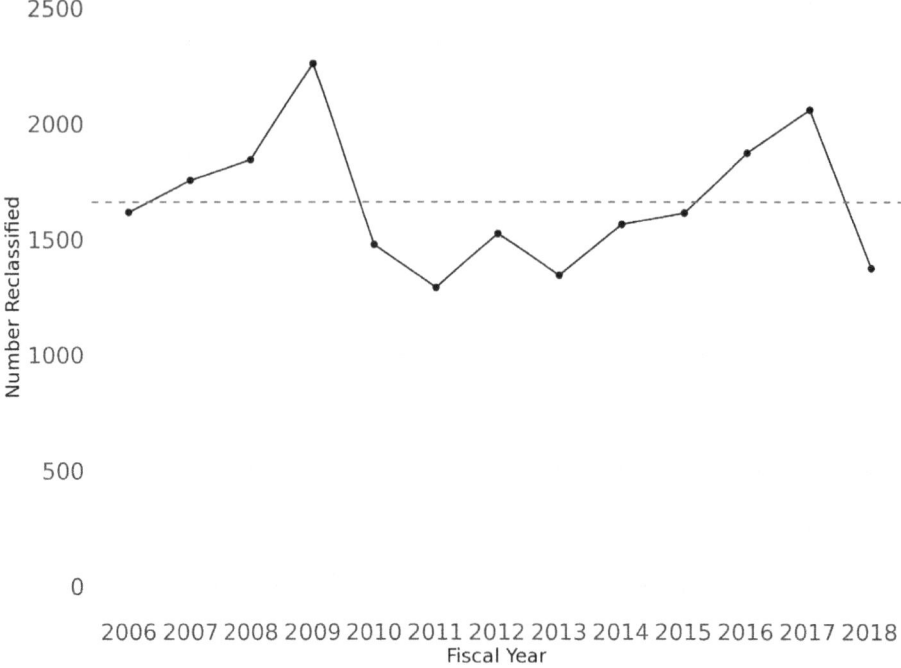

SOURCE: Authors' calculations based on USAF personnel data, FY 2006–2018.

Figure 1.2. Rate of Airmen Reclassified in Initial Skills Training, Fiscal Years 2006–2018

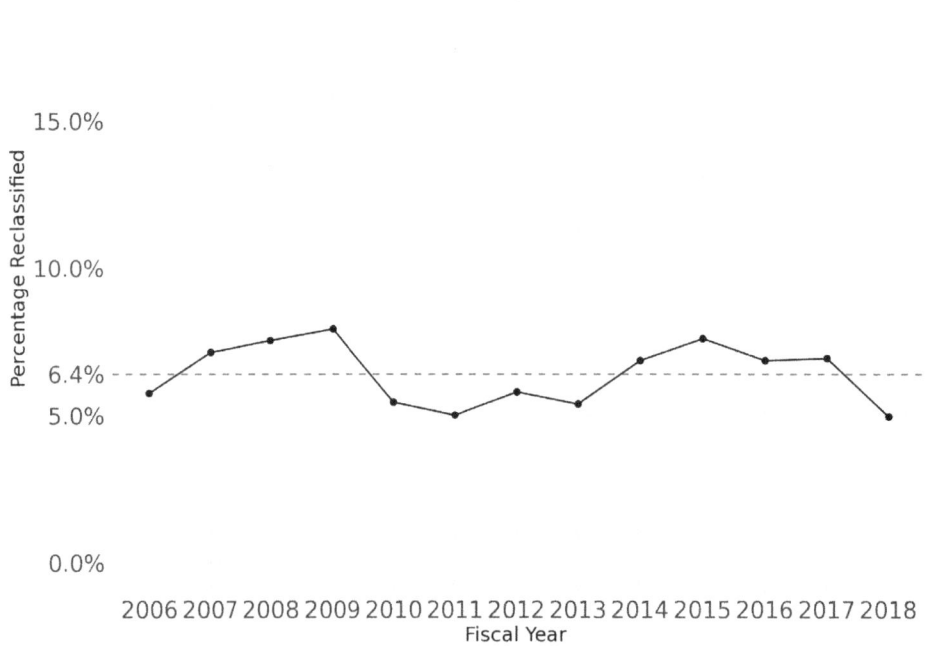

SOURCE: Authors' calculations based on USAF personnel data, FY 2006–2018.

One likely reason for the relatively steady rates shown in Figure 1.2 is that the number of reclassifications (shown in Figure 1.1) corresponds to the number of new trainees, such that as USAF accesses more people (who then go into training), more reclassifications occur.[5] This relationship between accessions and reclassifications may be partly due to USAF policies tied to increased end strength requirements (i.e., the need for more personnel to meet end strength may result in more trainees being reclassified instead of being removed from USAF).

Despite evidence that reclassification rates have not changed dramatically over the past several years, reclassifications still require USAF to expend resources. Reclassifications also reflect on the classification system, as some reclassifications may be due to errors or missed opportunities during classification. Therefore, understanding what affects reclassification requires understanding what affects classification. As depicted in Figure 1.3, the classification system accounts for USAF priorities (left side) and preferences of airmen (right side). The challenge for USAF is balancing priorities and preferences so that the classification system is efficient and effective. Imbalanced distributions of priorities may risk reclassification.

Figure 1.3. Classification System Including Air Force Priorities and Airmen Preferences

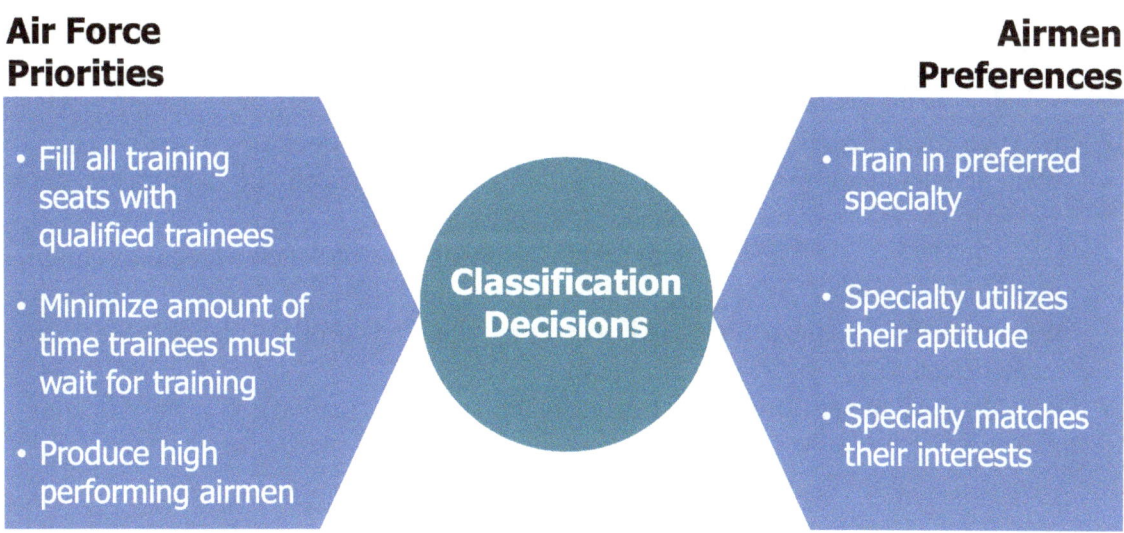

---

[5] Based on USAF personnel data from FY 2006–2018, the correlation between the number of new trainees and number of reclassifications by month within the same year is 0.68. A correlation of 0.50 or higher is considered a "large" effect size; see Jacob Cohen, "A Power Primer," *Psychological Bulletin*, Vol. 112, No. 1, 1992.

The balance of priorities in Figure 1.3 reflect current focus of the classification system, but this system has a long history that has evolved over time.[6] Today, USAF uses an algorithm known as "Job Spin" to make weekly AFS assignments at BMT, which includes inputs involving trainees' preferences and their minimum qualifications for specialties. Although Job Spin aims to balance many of the priorities in Figure 1.3, the model may fall short on optimal matching given the limited number of inputs used to assign airmen to jobs.

As newer analytic methods that can handle larger quantities of data, such as machine learning (ML) models, become more mainstream, USAF may benefit from another look at its classification and reclassification processes to determine if person-job match can be improved and done more efficiently.

Purpose and Approach

To understand and address the challenge of IST reclassification, and potentially improve both classification and reclassification, Headquarters Air Education and Training Command (AETC) asked RAND Project AIR FORCE (PAF) to explore options for improving processes to classify and reclassify enlisted airmen for IST. Here we present key findings, conclusions, and recommendations from an FY 2019 RAND PAF project on classification and reclassification of enlisted airmen in IST, with a focus on airmen who are on active duty and non–prior service (NPS).[7] The project addressed the following key questions:

- What enlisted classification and reclassification processes does USAF use?
- What potential gaps exist in USAF data to improve classification outcomes and reduce reclassifications?
- How do ML models compare with traditional statistical models for predicting training and career outcomes?
- What benefits (if any) could USAF realize by using optimization models for reclassification?
- Would USAF benefit from investments in ML for classification and reclassification?

---

[6] For a historical review of job matching in USAF, see Jacobina Skinner, Nancy Thompson, Kenneth Schwartz, and Johnny Weissmuller, *Air Force Personnel Research Issues: A Manager's Handbook*, San Antonio, Tex.: Operational Technologies Corp., 2007.

[7] We focus on active duty because the processes for career field assignment in the Air National Guard and Air Force Reserve are substantially different and less centralized. We also focus on NPS airmen because those who previously served (even if in another military service) would have some exposure to career field classification in the services, which would likely affect their preferences. A key challenge for USAF is to understand how to account for preferences of individuals without this prior exposure.

To address these key questions, we employed a mixed methods approach. Specifically, we conducted the following qualitative and quantitative analysis:

1. reviewed USAF and Department of Defense (DoD) policies and interviewed subject-matter experts (SMEs) in USAF to understand USAF enlisted classification and reclassification processes and identify relevant sources of data
2. reviewed and summarized relevant academic and policy research literature on the history of the USAF classification system and on tools that could be used for reclassification
3. conducted focus groups with airmen in select specialties to understand their experiences with AFS selection and knowledge of AFSs prior to IST, as well as experiences that might tie to IST outcomes (e.g., graduation, reclassification), with the goal of identifying potential gaps in USAF data that could improve classification and reduce reclassification
4. performed statistical analyses employing traditional regression models (e.g., logistic regression) as well as ML approaches; used 14 years of USAF recruit and personnel data to predict IST outcomes (graduation) and career outcomes (early separation, first-term reenlistment, and promotion to grade E-5)
5. developed a linear integer (optimization) model to test whether such a model could supplement or replace the current reclassification process by introducing efficiencies (cost savings) and effectiveness (i.e., sending airmen to AFSs where they will succeed).

We provide more details on our methodologies in later chapters and appendixes of this report.

Organization of This Report

This report has six additional chapters. The next chapter (Chapter 2) provides an overview of USAF classification and reclassification processes to acquaint the reader with how these processes work. The following chapter (Chapter 3) describes data that USAF has available for predicting IST and career outcomes (and associated challenges with the data). Chapter 4 provides the findings from our statistical modeling to predict IST and career outcomes. Chapter 5 offers the findings of the reclassification optimization modeling. Chapter 6 is a deep dive into the specialties for which we conducted focus groups. We conclude with Chapter 7, outlining key findings, their implications, and our recommendations for addressing USAF classification and reclassification.

2. Air Force Classification and Reclassification Processes

As noted in the previous chapter, the overarching goal of classification is to ensure that USAF matches airmen to the appropriate specialties in the right proportion to fulfill USAF's mission and strategic goals. Reclassification aims to retain airmen who have desirable qualifications, aptitudes, and attributes in USAF but who are either eliminated from IST or disqualified from an AFS following graduation (e.g., for not meeting Personnel Reliability Program requirements).[1] At least 1,200 NPS technical school trainees are reclassified annually.[2]

In this chapter we provide an overview of current processes by which USAF enlisted personnel are initially classified to specialties and are reclassified into other specialties after being eliminated from IST.[3] This chapter includes three main sections. First, we describe how classification begins prior to enlistment but continues through BMT. Next, we outline key features of the reclassification process. Finally, we provide observations about the classification and reclassification processes.

Initial Classification Process

The initial classification process, which proceeds from recruitment through technical training, has three main phases as depicted in Figure 2.1. The initial classification process begins, in the pre-enlistment phase, when individuals decide they want to join USAF. During this phase, the qualifications of applicants are assessed at recruitment, followed by tests and screening at the Military Entrance Processing Station (MEPS). Assuming applicants are successful in enlisting in USAF, they enter the second phase, the Delayed Entry Program (DEP), where they sign their enlistment contracts and await training. Following DEP, new airmen attend BMT, where they provide more information to USAF on their AFS preferences but also complete additional screening and testing to determine eligibility for different specialties. The screening, testing, and AFS preferences in BMT form the basis for USAF's use of an optimization model known as Job Spin, which assigns airmen to technical training seats for different specialties (i.e., IST), and is the final phase of the initial classification process. Technical training is where airmen gain skills and knowledge in their AFS before proceeding to their base assignments. Assuming airmen are

---

[1] U.S. Air Education and Training Command Instruction 36-2605, "Formal Flying Training Administration and Management," San Antonio, Tex.: Randolph Air Force Base, 2017; Department of Defense Manual 5210.42, *Nuclear Weapons Personnel Reliability Program*, Washington, D.C.: U.S. Department of Defense, 2018.

[2] Between FY 2006 and FY 2018, reclassifications ranged from a low of 1,291 in FY 2011 to a high of 2,260 in FY 2009. Most years have fewer than 2,000 reclassifications.

[3] Description of USAF classification and reclassification is based on information collected in FY 2019.

Figure 2.1. Phases of Initial Classification Process for Air Force Enlisted Specialties

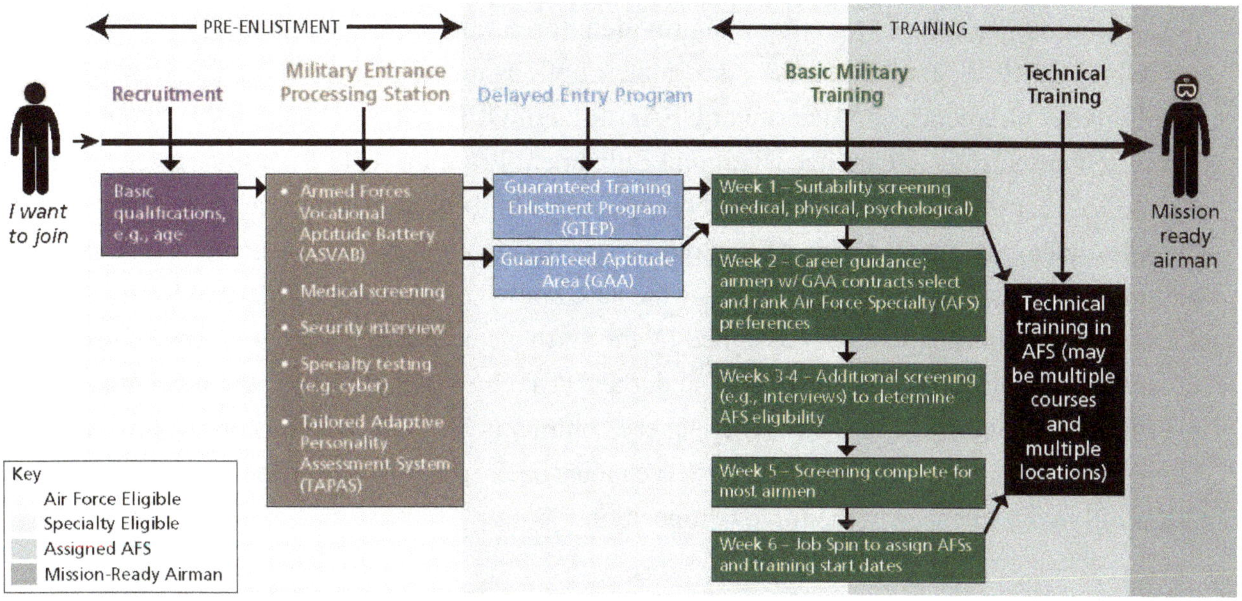

SOURCES: Bryan Sparkman, Technical Training Job Spin User's Manual, USAF-AETC, San Antonio, Tex.: Randolph Air Force Base, July 2010; R. S. McCloy, Rodney A. McCloy, Michael Ingerick, and William J. Strickland, *Towards an Advanced Personnel Accession System*, Alexandria, Va.: HumRRO, FR 08-40, 2008, p. 4; Subject Matter Expert Interviews, 2018–2019.

successful in completing technical training and do not have any additional disqualifiers, they are considered "mission ready" to enter their specialties after technical training.

We provide more details on the classification process in the following sections.

Before Enlistment

During the recruitment and MEPS phases, airmen discuss career options with recruiters and are screened to determine their eligibility to serve. USAF collects basic biographical data on recruits (i.e., enlisted applicants) such as their ages, citizenship/residency statuses, and education levels, as well as data about whether they meet minimum physical, conduct, and aptitude standards.[4] Recruiters complete part of this initial processing before applicants are more extensively screened at MEPS. While at MEPS, an applicant may take the Armed Forces Vocational Aptitude Battery (ASVAB), a measure of cognitive aptitude.[5] Along with the ASVAB, applicants take other tests, such as those required for entry into specific career fields (e.g., Electronic Data Processing Test [EDPT] for assessing aptitude in cyber), and they receive

---

[4] U.S. Air Force, "Meet Requirements," webpage, undated h.

[5] In some cases, recruits take the ASVAB prior to MEPS. See U.S. Air Force, "Frequently Asked Questions: Where Can I Take the ASVAB?" webpage, undated g.

medical screenings (e.g., blood tests). Applicants also begin their security interviews and provide fingerprints. Combined, these assessments and screenings help USAF determine who meets minimum standards for entry and provide information on AFS eligibility. [6]

While at MEPS, applicants also discuss their options for AFSs, which are based on minimum eligibility requirements. Enlistees enter USAF through DEP, during which they sign one of two kinds of contracts, the Guaranteed Training Enlistment Program (GTEP) or Guaranteed Aptitude Area (GAA, or open Aptitude Index). GTEP provides training in a particular AFS, whereas the open contract may guarantee an AFS in one of four broad aptitude areas—namely, mechanical, administrative, general, and electronics—which are known collectively as MAGE. Specific AFSs for GAA contracts are generally assigned by the sixth week of BMT.[7] In 2018, approximately 66 percent of enlistees shipped to BMT under a GTEP contract.[8] However, the percentage of GTEPs varies by AFS—for many AFSs, every contract is a GTEP, whereas only a few AFSs have no GTEPs.[9] USAF holds some AFS vacancies back from GTEP for assignment at BMT and to allow for changes in the force composition.

Basic Military Training

In the first week of BMT, airmen undergo initial screenings to assess their mental, medical, and physical health. For example, they undergo the Biographical Evaluation and Screening of Trainees program, which screens trainees for mental disorders.[10] They also have physical training (PT) assessments, as well as medical and dental examinations. In week two of BMT, trainees are given career guidance. Those with GAA contracts select and rank AFS preferences.[11] According to SMEs who are part of this process in BMT, in weeks three to four, additional screening is

---

[6] DoD sets some minimum standards for USAF in the aggregate, and other standards are written into U.S. law. For example, Title 10 of the U.S. Code, Chapter 31, requires a minimum score of 31 on the Armed Forces Qualification Test (AFQT) for enlistees without a high school diploma. (The AFQT is based on scores from four ASVAB subtests: arithmetic reasoning, work knowledge, paragraph comprehension, and mathematics knowledge.) In other cases, USAF sets minimum standards. For instance, USAF requires an AFQT score of at least 50 for applicants who possess an alternative educational credential such as a General Education Development certificate. The Air Force Recruiting Service Commander sometimes sets higher minimum AFQT scores than the Title 10 minimum, depending on recruiting market conditions.

[7] McCloy et al., 2008.

[8] Estimate based on analysis of USAF personnel data provided to RAND.

[9] Based on data provided by USAF to the RAND team, in FY 2019, only 5 percent of AFSs (which includes subspecialties known as "shreds") had no GTEPs available. Another 28 percent of AFSs offered between 20 and 50 percent GTEP, followed by 17 percent offering 60–90 percent GTEP, and about 24 percent with all spots being filled by GTEP contracts.

[10] Howard N. Garb, James M. Wood, Kristin Schneider, Monty Baker, and Wendy Travis, "Suitability Screening During Basic Military Training," *Military Psychology*, Vol. 25, No. 1, 2013.

[11] McCloy et al., 2008.

conducted to ensure trainees with GTEP contracts are still eligible for their assigned specialties and that airmen with GAA contracts are eligible for their preferred specialties. Screenings include sensitive skills interviews for security clearances and, for a select few AFSs (e.g., paralegal), interviews to determine AFS-specific interest and skills. AFSs requiring additional medical screening (e.g., flight physicals) are also conducted. By week five, AFS-specific screening is complete for most airmen.[12]

During week six of BMT, Second Air Force/Detachment 1 (2AF/Det 1) within AETC runs Job Spin, which is an optimization model that matches airmen to technical training (i.e., IST) seats. The model weighs several goals in the assignment process:

- fill the highest priority seats (infinite weight)
- assign airmen to their preferred specialties (50 percent)
- match characteristics held by airmen to those desired by AFSCs (e.g., high school course in physics) (30 percent)
- maximize individuals' ASVAB score (20 percent)[13]
- assign individuals to the earliest available class (0 percent).[14]

For airmen with GTEP contracts, the model merely assigns them to the next available training seats for the specialties to which their contracts apply. For airmen with open (i.e., non-GTEP) contracts, the model considers three inputs, which are differentially weighted and used to set the payoffs in the model:[15]

- desirable skills, including trainee characteristics (such as high school courses) that are associated with each AFS and are used to produce an aptitude index qualification[16]
- trainee's AFS preferences
- USAF needs and priorities.[17]

---

[12] According to SMEs from BMT, airmen who require top secret clearances may continue being screened during week five.

[13] Job Spin applies a weight to a variable that takes the difference between the individual's ASVAB score and a specialty's minimum ASVAB score, and then divides that difference by the following: (100 – specialty's ASVAB minimum score) × 100.

[14] Sparkman, 2010.

[15] Like the other military services, USAF needs to fill requirements across specialties, some of which might not be preferred by airmen. The tension between airmen preferences and service needs is an inherent part of the classification process.

[16] Prior to enlistment, the recruiter enters these into the Air Force Recruiting Information Support System (AFRISS), but the information is rescreened and validated during BMT.

[17] Sparkman, 2010.

By the end of BMT, trainees have been assigned to technical training seats corresponding to AFSs to which they have been assigned. If trainees do not meet the qualifications for their AFS, they can be reassigned to a new AFS.[18] (In rare cases, they may be separated from USAF.)

Technical Training

Assuming an airman meets the minimum requirements for a specialty and a seat is available within the time window specified by the Job Spin model, the airman attends technical training for the assigned specialty.[19] Most recruits have limited job experience before enlistment so USAF's training programs are designed to prepare airmen to fulfill the duties required of their specialties. Given differences in AFS duties, technical training pipelines vary in terms of length, number of courses, and minimum requirements to graduate. The length can vary from 6 to 72 weeks.[20]

If an airman successfully completes technical training and graduates, the airman is awarded a three-level status and is mission ready to enter their AFS.[21] If an airman does not successfully complete technical training, USAF can choose to remove the airman from service or reclassify the airman to another specialty. In the next section, we describe how USAF reclassifies airmen who do not complete technical training for a given AFS.

Reclassification During Initial Skills Training

Assuming USAF wishes to retain airmen who are eliminated from IST, the reclassification process is designed to assign those airmen to other AFSs for which they are at least minimally qualified. In addition to this qualification goal, USAF attempts to limit costs directly associated with the reclassification process, namely those required for moving an airman from one training location to another and time that the reclassified airman is "idle" (i.e., awaiting the new training after being eliminated from the previous training pipeline).

Reclassifying trainees to a new career path can happen for a number of reasons and at several points along the training pipeline. In most cases, trainees are reclassified following elimination from a training course. Figure 2.2 shows the top reasons that airmen have been eliminated from IST, during FY 2007–2018.

---

[18] For airmen with GTEP contracts, being reassigned is known as "GTEP release." Between 2006 and 2018, an average of 2.3 percent of airmen were GTEP-released. If airmen are GTEP-released before week six of BMT, they are put back into Job Spin for assignment.

[19] U.S. Air Force Manual 36-2100, *Military Utilization and Classification*, April 7, 2021.

[20] U.S. Air Force, "Technical Training," webpage, undated j.

[21] In USAF, personnel are awarded different skill levels to reflect their technical competence in their specialties as well as competence as airmen. USAF applies odd-numbered levels for enlisted personnel, ranging from 1 ("Helper," for those in initial training) to 9 (superintendent). (There is also a "0" code for career enlisted manager; see U.S. Air Force Manual 36-2100, p. 11.) An airman who is a 3-level is an "apprentice," meaning that person has met minimum requirements to perform in the specialty.

Figure 2.2. Reasons for Initial Skills Training Elimination, Fiscal Years 2007–2018

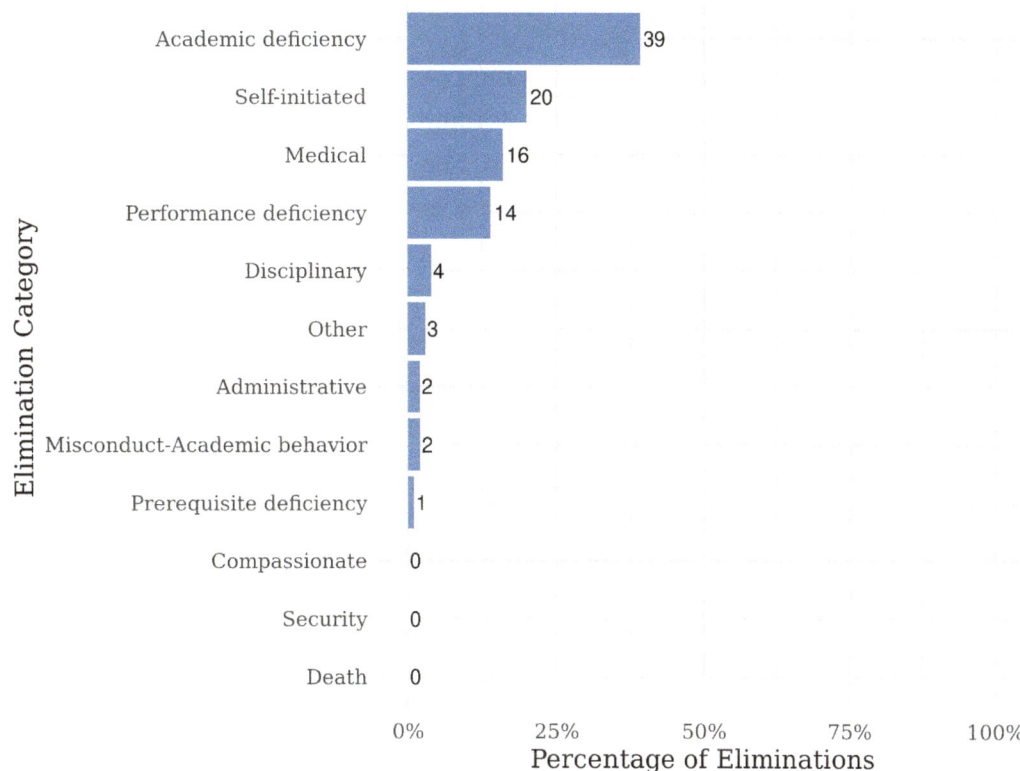

SOURCE: USAF personnel data provided to the RAND Corporation.
NOTE: Elimination categories are USAF generated. Percentages averaged across the years in the data.

As shown in Figure 2.2, academic deficiency (i.e., failing academic portions of training such as exams) is the most common reason, on average, that airmen are eliminated from IST. Self-initiated eliminations were second most common reason for elimination. They are available for airmen in specialties with significant medical and physical training requirements, such as aircrew and special warfare career fields.[22] Medical issues (e.g., unanticipated injury) and performance deficiency in training also eliminate over 10 percent of airmen, on average. The other categories tend to be less common, with less than 5 percent (on average) for any given category.[23]

Because trainees can be eliminated for different reasons, determining their minimal qualifications for another specialty (as well as the logistics of assigning them to new training pipelines) is a complex and layered process. Although the reclassification process is guided by manning and training guidance from Headquarters USAF and Headquarters AETC, most of the

---

[22] A vast majority (about 95 percent) of self-eliminations are from special warfare and combat support specialties.

[23] Some reasons for elimination might make it unlikely airmen would be reclassified. For example, misconduct that violates military ethical and legal regulations would likely be grounds for removal.

decisionmaking occurs in lower-level organizations in AETC, in particular, 2 AF/Det 1 and individual technical training schoolhouses/bases. The Air Force Personnel Center (AFPC) also has a role in that it processes the new assignments for reclassified airmen.[24]

The reclassification process begins when a trainee is about to be removed (or "eliminated") from the current technical training. If the trainee's training squadron commander decides the needs of USAF are better served by retaining the trainee in USAF, the trainee (known as an "eliminee") is recommended for reclassification.[25] Formally, the schoolhouse commander completes a reclassification package (AETC Form 125A) with comments that can include up to nine reclassification recommendations to specific specialties, with up to six recommendations from the eliminee and three from the training commander, depending on the practice in the particular schoolhouse and career field. There is also space on the form for commanders to provide comments that can be used to inform reclassification decisions.[26]

The next step of the reclassification process involves the Student Action Center, which completes AF Form 422 to provide medical updates on the airman who will be reclassified. Specifically, medical personnel at the training base conduct a medical screening of the airman and update the airman's status in terms of physical condition, upper extremities, lower extremities, hearing, vision, and psychiatric stability (PULHES), which is a military-wide system scored from 1 (normal capability) to 4 (most serious impediments).[27] In addition to medical screening, the airman can provide preferences for which AFSs to enter at the Student Action Center.[28] Once the forms needed for reclassification are complete, the Student Action Center submits the package to 2AF/Det 1.

On receipt of the reclassification package, 2AF/Det 1 reviews the airman's qualifications in a database known as Technical Training Management System—Job Match (TTMS-JM) to determine which AFSs the airman is minimally qualified to enter. 2AF/Det 1 also receives a list

---

[24] U.S. Air Force Manual 36-2100, 2021.

[25] Prior research shows that the broader human capital climate and USAF needs shape this decision. When end strength requirements are increasing, training schools are more likely to let a trainee retake a course or move to a new field. When USAF is making personnel reductions, schools are more likely to permit outright failure. See Lisa M. Harrington, Kathleen Reedy, John A. Ausink, Bart E. Bennett, Barbara Bicksler, Darrell D. Jones, and Daniel Ibarra, *Air Force Non-Rated Technical Training: Opportunities for Improving Pipeline Processes*, Santa Monica, Calif.: RAND Corporation, RR-2116-AF, 2017.

[26] According to SMEs from 2AF, commander comments tend to be general, rather than recommending specific specialties for airmen to enter. A comment might take the form of something like "Student was not able to handle technical information so recommend not sending to another technical career field."

[27] Each letter of PULHES presents a different aspect of the physical profile: physical condition (P), upper extremities (U), lower extremities (L), hearing (H), vision (eyes) (E), and psychiatric stability (S). See U.S. Air Force Instruction 48-123, *Medical Examinations and Standards*, November 5, 2013.

[28] According to SMEs at 2AF, it is not clear what guidance the airmen are given on which AFSs they are qualified to enter given that the Student Action Center may not have direct access to information about airman qualifications for different AFSs.

of training class seats that did not get filled in the weekly Job Spin run at BMT. 2AF/Det 1 compares the upcoming training seats in AFSs with available space with the reclassification packages and tries to give airmen one of their requested AFSs. The reclassification decision includes consideration of factors such as training seat availability, location (with a preference to keep trainees at current USAF bases), timing, and ASVAB scores (to ensure airmen are minimally qualified for AFSs being considered). In addition, top secret security clearances and flight physicals are limiting factors for some AFSs—in some cases because trainees cannot obtain them, and in other cases, SMEs say, because clearances are processed at distant bases, which would impose additional relocation costs.

Once the reclassed airman's new AFS is selected, 2AF/Det 1 forwards the package to AFPC for a change of assignment.[29] Specifically, AFPC changes the AFS in a military personnel database known as the Military Personnel Data System (MilPDS), loads the assignment to the new training location if necessary, and closes the case in the online system, MyPers. According to a SME, AFPC receives approximately 20 to 40 reclassification cases a week and aims to process them within three days, although temporary duty assignment reclassifications at a new base can take longer and skew the average. If a training date for a particular pipeline is fast approaching, 2AF/Det 1 will send an email to AFPC alerting them to prioritize the request.

AFPC's close-out of a reclassification case triggers a message back to 2AF/Det 1, which then notifies the training base where the assignment orders are published. The eliminee is then notified where and when the new training starts. If the eliminee misses the start date for training because of complications with a move or another type of delay, 2AF/Det 1 has to redo the reclassification decision.[30] However, most airmen who are reclassified are sent to only one AFS; two or more reclassifications are rare.[31]

Observations About Classification and Reclassification Processes

The classification and reclassification processes attempt to match enlistees with the right specialties and training in order to meet USAF's manpower needs. These processes are designed to provide flexibility to accommodate new career fields, changing demand, and variable numbers of enlistees. However, these processes also involve several steps, many of which are manual and can create inefficiencies and result in less-than-optimal matches of airmen to specialties.

---

[29] According to 2AF and AFPC SMEs, a case is opened in a database called MyPers. 2AF also sends an email to the AFPC team that processes the reclassification cases.

[30] This challenge of training delays creating inefficiencies is not limited to the reclassification process but can also create additional costs associated with airmen awaiting training. See Harrington et al., 2007.

[31] Based on data provided by USAF to RAND, only 1 to 2 percent of reclassifications are for airmen being reclassed the second time.

Observation 1: Each process operates like an airline reservation system. Classification and reclassification systems are designed to offer the first available training slots to airmen who meet minimum requirements for the associated specialties. As happens in an airline reservation system, seat availability can change within minutes. This creates a particular challenge for the reclassification process: 2AF/Det 1 has to "compete" with schoolhouses for open slots since schoolhouses use the same slots to assign students who need to retake portions of training (referred to as "washbacks").[32] As noted by a 2AF SME, "the training seats could be there for 10 minutes and then gone." 2AF might never see a seat that became available since schoolhouses hold back some seats for washbacks.

Observation 2: Both processes include challenges with transparency in decisionmaking. One transparency issue is that key actors in each process may not have a clear understanding of how other key actors are making decisions. In the case of classification, it may not be clear to those in BMT doing the follow-up screening of airmen how their recruiters decided to route them to GTEP AFSs, or how the airmen decided what they prefer. In the case of reclassifications, 2AF/Det 1 does not have full insight into how such decisions are made at the schoolhouse level (i.e., how the commander from the schoolhouse and associated schoolhouse staff decide a student should be reclassified after being eliminated from his or her current training pipeline). Another challenge is the lack of formal decisionmaking criteria (except for the Job Spin model). For example, there is no formal weighting scheme for reclassification; rather, 2AF/Det 1 uses general rules to decide where to route reclassified airmen. Specifically, 2AF/Det 1 considers training seat availability, location, and timing, *conditional* on the trainee having the qualifications for the specialty. Our project team did not find clear metrics guiding the cost-benefit decisions of these processes.

Observation 3: The Job Spin model is constrained by training times, and this presents challenges for hard-to-fill specialties. The Job Spin model offers a fixed number of seats in a short time horizon (i.e., one week) and is unable to consider airmen in future BMT cohorts to allocate seats in high-skill (and hard-to-fill) specialties.[33] Therefore, some highly skilled specialties may be full in one class but have available seats in the next. This variability in seat availability by specialty creates opportunity costs: airmen who would be good matches for highly skilled specialties at times when those specialties have limited seats available may be slotted to other (less well-matched) specialties with more seats available.

Observation 4: The dynamic nature of reclassifications makes it difficult to predict. Reclassification occurs for a number of reasons, some of which are difficult to predict. As shown

---

[32] Harrington et al., 2017.

[33] Under ideal conditions USAF would be able to evaluate all airmen from multiple cohorts for all assignments at the same time. Indeed, "it is well known and well documented that an organization using a batch process for job assignments will achieve more optimal person-job matches" (Skinner et al., 2017, p. 49).

in Figure 2.2, the top reasons for elimination include academic deficiency, self-eliminations (for special warfare AFSs), medical, and performance deficiency. An airman may not succeed in the training environment (e.g., fail a required test), or the airman may be ill-informed about career options, or the airman's preferences for career fields may change. The training environment itself, as well as unpredictable life events (e.g., family tragedies that require time away), can also result in reclassifications. These myriad reasons for reclassification make it challenging for the initial classification system to assign AFSs in a way to avoid reclassification, especially for things that are unpredictable.

3. Data Available for Predicting Air Force Training and Career Outcomes

One of the most significant trends across organizations in the private and public sectors during the twenty-first century is the rise of data science, a multidisciplinary field that uses processes, algorithms, and systems to extract knowledge and meaning from structured and unstructured data. The rise of data science is attributed to three interrelated developments: (1) the volume, variety, and velocity of data now available;[1] (2) the advent of new learning techniques to extract meaning from data;[2] and (3) the expansion of computational resources to apply these learning techniques at speed and scale. Despite the novelty of the concept, consensus has emerged about the utility of data science for describing past data, predicting future data, and prescribing courses of action.

The value of data science and of the contemporary modeling and prediction paradigms it uses have been demonstrated for a multitude of organizational functions, including human resource management functions.[3] A natural question, then, is whether USAF can also use these methods to improve selection and assignment of individuals to jobs to improve training outcomes (e.g., first-time pass rates), job outcomes (e.g., promotion timing), and career outcomes (e.g., first-term completion and reenlistment).[4] To address this question, this chapter provides an overview of the data USAF has available to develop contemporary models for classifying airmen. Chapter 4 follows with a discussion of the types of models that USAF could use and compares the performance of a select number of models using USAF data described in this chapter.

---

[1] *Volume* refers to the size of a data set in terms of either the number of records or the number of variables, *variety* refers to the distinct types of data being combined, and *velocity* refers to the amount of data being added regularly. See Dan J. Putka, Adam S. Beatty, and Matthew C. Reeder, "Modern Prediction Methods: New Perspectives on a Common Problem," *Organizational Research Methods*, Vol. 21, No. 3, 2018.

[2] Broadly, these techniques fall under the heading of ML, which is defined as "[a] program or system that builds (trains) a predictive model from input data. The system uses the learned model to make useful predictions from new (never-before-seen) data drawn from the same distribution as the one used to train the model. Machine learning also refers to the field of study concerned with these programs or systems" (Google, "Machine Learning," webpage, January 22, 2019).

[3] Stefan Strohmeier and Franca Piazza, "Domain Driven Data Mining in Human Resource Management: A Review of Current Research," *Expert Systems with Applications*, Vol. 40, No. 7, 2013.

[4] Amy C. Hooper, Cheryl Paullin, Dan J. Putka, and William S. Strickland, *An Empirical Analysis of Reasons for Attrition Among First-Term Airmen in the United States Air Force*, Alexandria, Va.: Human Resources Research Organization, 2008.

Air Force Personnel Data Sources

USAF collects data on individuals as part of its personnel management processes, beginning with recruitment and continuing through separation (or retirement). Depending on where individuals are in their careers, data are collected and recorded by different people in different offices and entered into different USAF personnel systems. The quality of these data varies widely in terms of relevance and completeness. Some measures (e.g., cognitive aptitude) have been collected for several decades and have been explored in prior research.[5] Others are in the development stage. When viewed in aggregate, these data provide an opportunity to explore associations between a large number of factors associated with individuals when they are applicants or trainees and their training, performance, and career outcomes.

Using personnel selection research as a framework, we reviewed available predictor and outcome measures contained in USAF personnel systems and created a relational database that combined records from NPS, active-duty enlisted personnel across seven sources (Table 3.1).[6] As a starting point, we used data in Technical Training Management System (TTMS) on airmen who completed IST between FY 2005 and FY 2019. For those individuals, we compiled a set of predictor variables that were collected before enlistment and recorded in the Air Force Recruiting Information Support System—Total Force (AFRISS-TF). In cases where variables were missing for an individual, we filled them in using values captured at later dates in the AETC Decision Support System (ADSS) and Active Enlisted Personnel Extracts (AAE). We included scores from the Tailored Adaptive Personality Assessment System (TAPAS) when available.[7] Finally, we used data from TTMS and AAE to calculate technical training outcomes, first-term outcomes, and retention outcomes for each individual.

In the following sections, we describe the different categories of data available in USAF personnel systems. Figure 3.1 illustrates the general predictor and outcome categories that we reviewed. We begin with a discussion of outcomes since those are criteria against which airmen success would be measured. We then follow with a discussion of categories of predictors.

---

[5] James A. Earles and Malcolm James Ree, "The Predictive Validity of the ASVAB for Training Grades," *Educational and Psychological Measurement*, Vol. 52, No. 3, 1992; Thomas Manacapilli, Carl F. Matthies, Louis W. Miller, Paul Howe, P. J. Perez, Chaitra M. Hardison, H. G. Massey, Jerald Greenberg, Christopher Beighley, and Carra S. Sims, *Reducing Attrition in Selected Air Force Training Pipelines*, Santa Monica, Calif.: RAND Corporation, TR-955-AF, 2012; Mark R. Rose, Gregory G. Manley, and Johnny J. Weissmuller, *Development of Two-And Three-Factor Classification Models for Air Force Battlefield Airmen (BA) and Related AFSs*, AFCAPS-TR-2013-0007, San Antonio, Tex.: Air Force Personnel Center, Randolph Air Force Base, 2013.

[6] See Appendix A for a brief overview of relevant predictors and outcomes used in personnel selection research.

[7] Although more TAPAS data are available, only Version 5 has been properly normed for analysis. For this reason, the majority of airmen included in our data set did not have interpretable TAPAS scores. Therefore, TAPAS was excluded from the full model evaluations described in Chapter 4.

Table 3.1. Data Sources, Date Ranges, and Records and Variables

Database	Description	Date Range[a]	Records Retained
AFRISS-TF	USAF recruiting service's central tool to track and facilitate recruiting operations	FY04–FY18	370,374
ADSS	Cube-based web application for accessing AETC data	FY06–FY18	349.350
BMT Personnel Actions	Records performance and status for all recruits during basic military training	FY05–FY19	348,075
TTMS	Records student course performance and status for all technical trainees	FY05–FY19	369,853
AAE	Monthly extracts from MilPDS with information on active duty enlisted personnel	FY04–FY18	358,160
Job satisfaction	Job satisfaction survey data provided by AETC/AAE	FY09–FY18	58,363
TAPAS[b]	TAPAS data provided by AFPC	FY14–FY18	17,777

[a] Date ranges include fiscal years with any records.
[b] Data retained for TAPAS Version 5.

Figure 3.1. Analytical Linkages Between Predictors and Outcomes

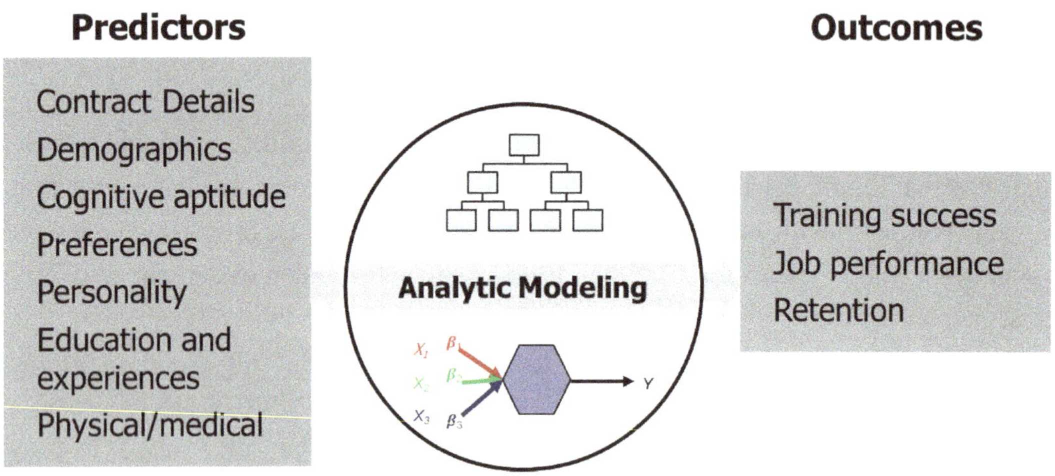

Training and Career Outcomes Measured by the U.S. Air Force

USAF uses three major categories of outcomes for NPS service enlisted personnel:

1. **Training success:** AETC lists metrics tracked by USAF to evaluate the operational performance of airmen during technical training.[8] These include training outcomes such as whether an individual graduates from a course, is washed back after failing to complete a section of a course, or is eliminated for academic failure or a multitude of other reasons. These metrics also include training progress, such as unit grades and end of course grades.[9]
2. **Job performance:** This can be assessed in a variety of ways. For example, performance can be indirectly assessed by tracking time to achieve promotions and skill upgrades.[10] Performance can also be directly measured using supervisor ratings from Enlisted Performance Reports (EPRs).[11]
3. **Retention:** The primary retention measures pertain to whether an individual completes his or her first enlisted term and whether he or she reenlists.[12]

Some of these measures can be extracted directly from databases. For example, TTMS contains training outcomes by individual and course. Other measures can be extracted directly from databases but must be rescaled. For instance, EPRs provide numerical ratings by individual, but rating scales and criteria have changed over time and so must be transformed. Finally, some of these measures must be derived from one or more variables. For example, we identified early separation based on the relationship between an individual's date of enlistment, date of separation, and initial term of enlistment (TOE).

We used TTMS and AAE to derive four outcome measures that cut across the three primary categories. *Complete technical training* is whether an individual completed the technical training associated with their first assigned specialty. *Complete first term* is whether an individual completed his or her first enlisted term, as opposed to separating more than three months early. *Promotion to E-5 in first term* is whether an individual reached E-5 in his or her first term.

---

[8] U.S. Air Force Manual 36-2100, 2021.

[9] Training outcomes are included by individual and course in TTMS. Because a technical training pipeline is comprised of multiple courses, outcomes must be evaluated for all courses to determine whether an individual was a first-time graduate, whether he or she washed back, or whether he or she was eliminated.

[10] To determine the timing of promotions and skill upgrades, we used date variables contained in AAE. We also used data contained in AAE to compute reasons for why individuals were nondeployable (e.g., legal, physical, or administrative).

[11] EPRs were inconsistently available, and the manner in which raters are instructed to assign ratings has changed in recent years, complicating their longitudinal use.

[12] To determine whether individuals completed their first enlisted term and whether they choose to reenlist, we used data contained in AAE.

Reenlist is whether an individual reenlisted.[13] Table 3.2 shows the percentage of individuals with positive outcomes for each measure.

Table 3.2. Outcome Measures Retained for Analysis

Outcome Measure	Positive (Percentage)
Complete technical training	90.3
Complete first term	70.1
Promotion to E-5 in first term[a]	34.9
Reenlist	41.7

[a] Sixteen percent of individuals with a 4-year initial term of enlistment reach E-5, versus 50 percent of individuals with a 6-year enlistment.

Available Predictor Measures of Airmen Training and Career Outcomes

USAF could use a vast number of predictors to assign NPS enlisted personnel to jobs.[14] These fall into seven categories:

1. **Contract details:** Contract details include TOE, entry pay grade, and GTEP. GTEP refers to individuals with guaranteed jobs at the time of enlistment. Although contract details are not individual attributes per se, they give important context for interpreting individuals' outcomes.
2. **Demographics:** Demographics have consistently been shown to relate to training and career outcomes.[15] Although it would be unethical to base job placement on protected category status such as race, gender, ethnicity, and religion, it is nonetheless important to understand how these variables relate to outcomes.
3. **Cognitive aptitude:** Cognitive aptitudes are captured primarily by the ASVAB, which comprises eight domain-specific subtests that can be combined to create composite scores aligned to knowledge, skills, and abilities needed for different USAF career fields. ASVAB subtest and composite scores have been shown to be predictive of overall military success

---

[13] The relational database contained other outcome measures including enlisted performance reviews, IST grades, job satisfaction survey data, number and percentage of deployable days, time to achieve each rank, and time to achieve each skill level. We focused on the selected set because they were fairly complete, they varied across individuals, and they are highly relevant to USAF's job assignment goals. Promotion to E-5 requires a minimum of 36 months of time in service, 6 months of time in grade, and a 5-skill level. Yet selections for promotion to E-5 are made using the weighted airman promotion system which, among other things, assigns additional points for time in grade. Promotion to E-5 within the first enlisted term, though not exceptional, is by no means pervasive.

[14] AFPC, *Air Force Enlisted Classification Directory (AFECD): The Official Guide to the Air Force Enlisted Classification Codes*, Randolph, Tex.: Air Force Public Affairs Agency, April 30, 2018.

[15] William E. Alley, Leticia J. Pachecho, David B. Birkelbach, Kenneth L. Schwartz, and Johnny J. Weissmuller, *Modeling Individual Performance Criteria in the Air Force*, AFCAPS-FR-2010-0015, San Antonio, Tex.: Operational Technologies Corp., 2007.

and success in specific career fields.[16] Other cognitive aptitude tests, such as the Defense Language Aptitude Battery (DLAB), are administered on a limited basis to individuals considered for specific jobs.

4. **Preferences:** Preferences provide a proxy for vocational interest—that is, whether an individual's interests fit with the tasks and environment associated with his or her assigned job. However, preferences are a weak proxy because they depend on the individual both knowing about the tasks and environment associated with a job and accurately evaluating the extent to which these overlap with his or her interests. New instruments such as the Air Force Work Interest Navigator (AF-WIN) may provide a more valid measure of vocational interest, but they are not yet widely deployed.[17]

5. **Personality:** Personality tests such as TAPAS have been found to add predictive validity beyond measures of cognitive aptitudes and vocational interest.[18] However, like measures of vocational interest, they are not yet widely deployed.

6. **Education and experience:** Education and experience entail elements of cognitive aptitude, vocational interest, and personality.[19] For example, educational attainment depends in part on cognitive ability, but it also depends on personality factors such as adaptability and commitment to achieving a goal.[20] Additionally, a chosen field of study and high school courses completed may reflect an individual's vocational interests. Finally, in addition to the information they provide about an individual, a particular set of experiences may uniquely qualify the individual for certain jobs.

7. **Physical/medical:** Certain physical and medical conditions may limit an individual's ability to perform certain jobs. These are captured in the PULHES grading system. Other anthropometric variables such as height and weight are associated with completing basic military training, job performance, and deployability.[21]

Of the potentially vast number of predictor variables, we retained ones that might reasonably be expected to affect first-term enlistment outcomes (Table 3.3). Many of these variables have been used before in prediction models of first-term outcomes, and many are used to set minimum requirements for jobs. Completeness refers to the percentage of individuals with a reported value

---

[16] Thomas R. Carretta, "Predictive Validity of the Armed Services Vocational Aptitude Battery for Several U.S. Air Force Enlisted Training Specialties," Air Force Research Laboratory/Human Effectiveness Directorate, Dayton, Ohio: Wright-Patterson Air Force Base, 2014.

[17] James F. Johnson, Sophie Romay, and Laura Barron, "Air Force Work Interest Navigator (AF-WIN) to Improve Person-Job Match: Development, Validation, and Initial Implementation," *Military Psychology*, Vol. 32, No. 1, 2019.

[18] Stephen Stark, Oleksandr S. Chernyshenko, Fritz Drasgow, Christopher D. Nye, Leonard A. White, Tonia Heffner, and William L. Farmer, "From ABLE to TAPAS: A New Generation of Personality Tests to Support Military Selection and Classification Decisions," *Military Psychology*, Vol. 26, No. 3, 2014.

[19] Christopher M. Berry, Melissa L. Gruys, and Paul R. Sackett, "Educational Attainment as a Proxy for Cognitive Ability in Selection: Effects on Levels of Cognitive Ability and Adverse Impact," *Journal of Applied Psychology*, Vol. 91, No. 3, 2006.

[20] Michael G. Rumsey and Jane M. Arabian, "Military Enlistment Selection and Classification: Moving Forward," *Military Psychology*, Vol. 26, No. 3, 2014.

[21] John Cawley and Johanna Catherine Maclean, "Unfit for Service: The Implications of Rising Obesity for US Military Recruitment," *Health Economics*, Vol. 21, No. 11, 2012.

for the corresponding variable. Appendix B provides further details on these variables, including the percentage of individuals with positive outcomes for each measure and the completeness of the measures across all individuals.

It is also important to model these predictors in the context of differences among the specialties. One way to do this would be to produce a model for each specialty, which assumes that the predictor variables can affect the outcomes uniquely within each specialty. Alternatively, we can cluster the specialties by their codes (i.e., by AFSC) and allow the predictors to have different effects on the outcome only within the clusters. This is akin to the current MAGE categorization, which divides AFSCs into four groups and assumes similarity within the groups. In our modeling efforts we group the specialties using three more granular approaches to clustering AFSCs, based on size, positive outcome rate, and global careers clusters.[22]

Table 3.3. Predictor Variables Retained for Further Analysis

Continuous Predictor	Category	Mean	Completeness (Percentage)
Age at enlistment	Demographics	20.5	65.2
Mechanical aptitude composite (ASVAB)	Cognitive aptitude	63.5	100
Administrative aptitude composite (ASVAB)	Cognitive aptitude	70.0	100
General aptitude composite (ASVAB)	Cognitive aptitude	67.5	100
Electronics aptitude composite (ASVAB)	Cognitive aptitude	69.8	100
AFQT score	Cognitive aptitude	68.7	100
Arithmetic reasoning subtest (ASVAB)	Cognitive aptitude	55.5	94.4
Auto-shop information subtest (ASVAB)	Cognitive aptitude	49.5	94.4
Electrical information subtest (ASVAB)	Cognitive aptitude	53.8	94.4
Mechanical comprehension subtest (ASVAB)	Cognitive aptitude	55.3	94.4
Math knowledge subtest (ASVAB)	Cognitive aptitude	57.0	94.4
Paragraph comprehension subtest (ASVAB)	Cognitive aptitude	55.3	94.4
Word knowledge subtest (ASVAB)	Cognitive aptitude	53.4	94.4
Height	Physical/medical	68.3 inches	94.3
Weight	Physical/medical	154.4 lbs.	94.3

Categorical Predictor	Category	Mode	Completeness (Percentage)
Ethnicity	Demographics	White	97
Gender	Demographics	Male	97.7
Marital status	Demographics	Single	97
Number of dependents	Demographics	0	97
Race	Demographics	White	97
Religion	Demographics	Evangelical protestant	71.1

---

[22] *Global career clusters* refer to functional communities with similar occupational mission focus, organizational function, job context, and work activities, as defined by AF-WIN. Clusters are provided in Table B.3.

Categorical Predictor	Category	Mode	Completeness (Percentage)
Academic	Demographics	Some college	90.4
Term of enlistment	Contract	6 years	100
Entry pay grade	Contract	E1	91.7
First language	Education/Experience	English	93.6
Algebra	Education/Experience	Yes	94.4
Biology	Education/Experience	Yes	94.4
Chemistry	Education/Experience	Yes	94.4
English	Education/Experience	Yes	94.4
Geometry	Education/Experience	Yes	94.4
Physics	Education/Experience	No	94.4
Trigonometry	Education/Experience	No	94.4
Typing	Education/Experience	Yes	94.4
Physical profile: physical capacity or stamina	Physical/Medical	Pass	92.5
Physical profile: upper extremities	Physical/Medical	Pass	92.6
Physical profile: lower extremities	Physical/Medical	Pass	92.6
Physical profile: hearing and ears	Physical/Medical	Pass	92.6
Physical profile: eyes	Physical/Medical	Pass	92.6
Physical profile: psychiatric	Physical/Medical	Pass	92.6
Strength aptitude test	Physical/Medical	100 lbs.	92.5
1st job preference	Preferences	3P0X1	93.7
2nd job preference	Preferences	2A3X3	50
3rd job preference	Preferences	2A3X3	48.7
4th job preference	Preferences	9TG43[a]	47.8
Junior ROTC	Education/Experience	No	86.4
Peace Corps	Education/Experience	No	35.1

NOTE: We group predictors into those measured on a continuous scale versus those measured in categories (e.g., algebra refers to whether an airman took algebra in high school).
[a] 9TG43 denotes an open contract based on General (G) composite score and jobs.

Data Quality and Access Limitations

While compiling data for this project, we identified several limitations in the quality of the data. We also ran into challenges accessing certain sources of data. In Table 3.4, we briefly summarize the data quality and access issues we identified. This table does not reflect all potential quality and access challenges; rather, it illustrates the range of issues we encountered.

USAF records a vast amount of data about NPS enlisted personnel, including information about their aptitudes, education, personalities, and interests. But USAF also discards some potentially useful information about airmen qualifications. For example, the information used to assign airmen to AFSCs at BMT is retained in a personnel data system (i.e., TTMS-JM) only until graduation from IST. Once the airman has graduated, the information is removed from TTMS-JM, and no archive is retained. Although some of the data can be found in other systems, some variables (e.g., AFSC preferences provided at BMT, desired qualifications, and so on) are

Table 3.4. Air Force Personnel Data Quality and Access Limitations

Limitation	Example
Precision and accuracy of data entry	Skill-level award dates not always updated
Inconsistency of data collection	High school courses recorded only if desired by AFSC
Change in variable names and/or meaning over time	Enlisted performance records
Discarded data	TTMS-JM data used by Job Spin discarded after students graduate technical training
Digital capture not available for some sources	AF Form 125As retained as PDFs
Data access limitations	Air Traffic Control Scenario Test (ATC-ST) is maintained on one machine and data are kept in only one siloed database at AFPC

difficult or impossible to replicate. Other data limitations reflect the accuracy and completeness of records. For example, AF-WIN is optional and was only recently implemented in May 2018. In other cases, assessments (e.g., TAPAS) require further processing to ensure scores are comparable across different versions that have been used over time. Combined, these and other issues listed in Table 3.4 could limit the full benefits of using more advanced analytic models (e.g., ML models presented in Chapter 4) to classify airmen.

A relatively underexplored aspect of these data is using individual-level prediction probabilities for different outcomes to match individuals to jobs. In the next chapter, we use a range of ML techniques to identify these dependencies and to use predictive models to improve the assignment of individuals to jobs.

4. Models to Predict Success

In this chapter, we briefly review approaches to classification. Here, we use the term *classification* in the statistical sense to describe the prediction of an outcome, rather than in the functional sense of assigning an airman to a career field. We begin with general linear models (GLMs), a traditional approach, and we move on to increasingly flexible contemporary ML approaches. We then apply both traditional and more flexible ML approaches to the problem of predicting training and job and career outcomes for NPS enlisted personnel.

An Overview of Modern Prediction Methods

Organizational scientists have begun to use data science tools to address issues related to personnel selection and performance prediction. This entails more than just applying existing analytical methods to larger data sets; rather, it requires adopting a different perspective and new methods for learning from data. Historically, data modeling has been the prevailing statistical culture.[1] This culture assumes that outcomes are produced by an underlying model, which can be inferred from data. Recently, a new algorithmic modeling culture has become increasingly prevalent. This culture does not try to infer the underlying model, but instead tries to predict its outcomes given a set of inputs.

The shift from data modeling to algorithmic modeling usually involves exploring additional statistical methods besides GLMs. The advantages of these approaches are threefold. First, most of these methods can take a large number of variables relative to the number of observations and produce a predictive model that balances the trade-off between parsimony and explanatory power.[2] Second, some of these methods can detect item interactions and nonlinear relations not specified in advance. Third, some of these methods average over an ensemble of underlying models to mitigate the risk of accepting a single incorrect model. These are a few of the technical reasons for considering algorithmic models. An equally compelling reason is the repeated demonstration that these methods can perform extremely well in prediction tasks.

---

[1] Leo Breiman, "Statistical Modeling: The Two Cultures," *Statistical Science*, Vol. 16, No. 3, 2001.

[2] This is sometimes called the *variance-bias dilemma*. An overly complex model may account for all data in the sample yet make highly variable predictions. Conversely, an overly simple model may fail to account for data in the sample and may underpredict future samples. In both cases, the result is the same: poor prediction of future outcomes. Several statistical learning methods offer meta-parameters that can be tuned, manually or automatically, to manage the trade-off between parsimony and complexity. See Stuart Geman, Elie Bienenstock, and René Doursat, "Neural Networks and the Bias/Variance Dilemma," *Neural Computation*, Vol. 4, No. 1, 1992.

The statistical methods associated with algorithmic models come with drawbacks as well. Some of these drawbacks, like the tendency toward overfitting, can be addressed through technical means. Other drawbacks, such as potential lack of interpretability and "fairness" (i.e., whether an algorithm systematically disadvantages a subset of individuals based on extraneous factors), are more fundamental. We return to these drawbacks and to how USAF can manage them in Chapter 7.

Types of Machine Learning

The purpose of ML approaches is to estimate a function that maps inputs to outputs. Once learned, the function can be used to predict outcomes for a given set of inputs; for example, whether an airman with certain attributes will complete his or her IST.[3] The performance of the ML approach is typically evaluated in one of two ways. First, how well does it account for existing data (i.e., *quality of fit*)? Second, how well does it account for future data (i.e., *quality of prediction*)?

Improved prediction is the ultimate goal for an organization. Achieving high quality of fit is necessary, but not sufficient for achieving high quality of prediction. A model that systematically fails to account for some existing data is said to be biased. This bias will affect prediction. Conversely, an overly complex model may account for all existing data but may be highly sensitive to small changes in inputs. The model is said to suffer from high variance, which will also affect prediction. The major advantage of contemporary ML approaches is their ability to use all available predictor variables to reduce bias, while managing complexity to reduce variance.

The types of algorithmic modeling approaches for ML are extremely diverse, and include

- **General linear models:** GLMs assume that the outcome is a linear combination of the predictor variables. GLMs estimate the values of coefficients that minimize the sum of squared differences between predicted and actual outcomes. Additional terms can be added to the GLM to account for nonlinear relationships between predictor variables and outcomes and for interactions between variables.
- **Shrinkage methods:** Given a large number of predictor variables, some of which are linearly related, GLMs may produce highly uncertain coefficient estimates. This uncertainty reduces prediction accuracy. Shrinkage methods such as ridge and lasso regression apply a penalty to large coefficient estimates. Reducing the magnitude of coefficients reduces model variance and improves prediction accuracy.

---

[3] The statistical literature distinguishes between "regression" and "classification" problems. The former involves predicting continuously scaled outcomes (e.g., technical training test scores or length of service), and the latter involves predicting categorical outcomes (e.g., first-time completion of technical training versus completing with washback versus failure to complete). A special case of classification problems involves binary outcomes, such as whether an individual completes technical training or whether he or she decides to reenlist. See Trevor Hastie, Robert Tibshirani, and Jerome Friedman, *The Elements of Statistical Learning: Data Mining, Inference and Prediction*, New York: Springer, 2015.

- **Classification and regression tree (CART):** CART methods find a sequence of yes/no decision rules useful for classifying instances. They involve (a) identifying the single predictor variable that produces the best separation of outcome cases; (b) separating cases based on that predictor variable; and (c) iteratively deepening the tree by selecting additional predictor variables to separate cases into increasingly homogenous groups. The final trees can be highly complex and case-specific, and so a pruning step is taken to remove splits in the data that only yield marginal gains.
- **Bagging, random forest (RF):** CART methods suffer from high variance; given slightly different training data, they may learn very different trees. A collection of techniques has been developed to reduce the variance of CART. Bagging involves learning multiple trees from different subsets of training data. RFs further involve learning multiple trees from different subsets of *variables* in training data. Both techniques average predictions across the ensemble of learned trees.
- **Bayesian additive regression tree (BART):** Like bagging and RFs, BART generates predictions using an ensemble of learned trees. A Bayesian procedure is implemented to control the model fit.
- **Support vector machine (SVM):** SVMs represent training examples in a high-dimensional space. Dimensions correspond to the set of predictor variables, and the placement of a training example is determined by its value along each dimension. The SVM learns a decision boundary to separate training examples based on their associated outcomes.
- **Neural network (NN):** NNs are made up of interconnected nodes organized into layers. The input layer takes values of predictor variables as inputs, and the output layer produces the final response. NNs typically have one or more hidden layers that transform values as they are passed from the input to the output layer. Using a learning procedure such as back-propagation, NN learns a set of connection weights between nodes that produce correct responses for different input values.

These methods give organizational researchers powerful tools for predicting outcomes. Increasingly flexible methods may be called for, given the number and characteristics of predictor variables, and the manner in which they relate to outcomes. Notwithstanding their potential, these methods also have limitations. Most fundamental is the trade-off between flexibility and interpretability (Figure 4.1). Given enough data and suitable values for tuning parameters, ML methods with a high degree of flexibility may have highest prediction accuracy. Yet it may be difficult to understand why they generate the predictions that they do. Alternatively, methods with a low degree of flexibility may have lower prediction accuracy, yet may be easy to understand. A subset of methods, such as shrinkage methods, contribute simultaneously to flexibility and interpretability.

All these methods vary with respect to several other technical and performance characteristics (Table 4.1). *Bias-variance trade-off* describes the ability of the approach to handle a large number of predictors relative to the number of observations, and nonlinearity/interactions describes the ability of the approach to handle nonlinear relationships and interactions between predictors and

Figure 4.1. Interpretability and Flexibility of Machine Learning Approaches

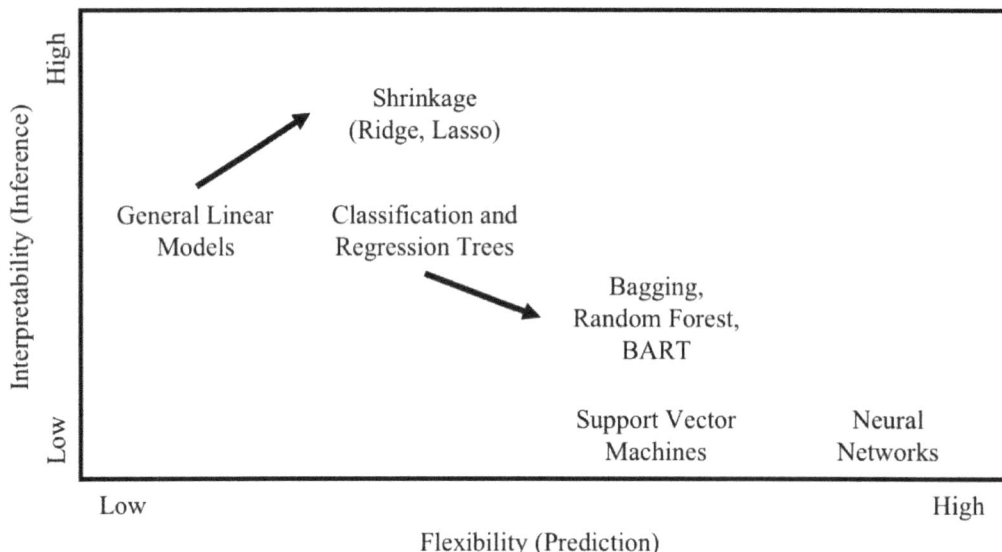

Table 4.1. Summary and Characteristics of Machine Learning Approaches

Method	Bias-Variance Tradeoff	Nonlinearity/ Interactions	Ensemble Prediction	Interpretable	Compute Speed
GLM	−	−	−	+	+
Ridge/lasso	+	−	−	+	+
Classification and regression trees	−	+	−	+	+
Bagging/RFs	+	+	+	−	+
SVMs	+	+	−	−	−
NNs	+	+	−	−	−

NOTE: The + symbol means that the method is relatively strong at addressing the characteristic; the − symbol means that the method is relatively weak at addressing the characteristic.

outcomes.[4] *Ensemble prediction* indicates whether the method predicts outcomes based on some combination of simpler models. *Interpretable* describes whether the reasons for the method's predictions are easily understood. Finally, *compute speed* refers to the time that the method needs to learn patterns in the data. Although these characteristics provide some guidance as to whether a particular method will perform well for a particular problem, the standard approach in data science is to try all methods and to retain the one that maximizes predictive performance.

---

[4] Despite having low flexibility relative to other methods, GLMs are still prone to overfitting given a large number of predictors and a small number of observations. Different forms of regularization in Ridge and Lasso regression can reduce variance in these cases.

Application of Machine Learning Techniques to Classification

Data science has been applied to myriad topics in human resource management (HRM), including personnel selection, career development, performance management, and compensation planning.[5] These applications have touched on all of the ML methods and associated algorithms contained in Table 4.1. For example, one seminal study used a variety of decision-tree approaches to predict performance of employees in a high-technology company.[6] The variables most predictive of job performance were school tier, recruitment channel, type of degree, and experience. These variables also predicted retention, although individuals' jobs within the company dominated continuation outcomes.

A subsequent study compared CART and NN with GLM for predicting employee productivity. CART and NN were more powerful in identifying high performance employees.[7] More recently, a study showed the power of tree-based approaches and shrinkage methods for predicting police officer and teacher performance relative to current hiring systems.[8] These studies exemplify an ever-growing body of research comparing the performance of various ML approaches relative to one another and to existing organizational practices.[9]

ML approaches may be especially useful when the number of predictor variables is large relative to the number of observations. For example, one study used 83 personality and motivation–related items to predict national order of merit list scores for individuals in the U.S. Army's Reserve Officer Training Corps.[10] Shrinkage methods, ensemble tree-based approaches, and a variety of other ML methods outperformed GLM when the size of the training sample was small, but differences disappeared when the sample was large. This demonstrates the ability of ML approaches to use data from all available predictor variables while still managing model complexity.

The development of new tools and methods for capturing predictor variables and quantifying performance have further enabled applications of data science to HRM. For example, computational linguistics have been used to extract information from resumes and company communications,

---

[5] Peter Cappelli, Prasanna Tambe, and Valery Yakubovich, "Artificial Intelligence in Human Resources Management: Challenges and a Path Forward," *Social Science Research Network*, 2018.

[6] Chen-Fu Chien and Li-Fei Chen, "Data Mining to Improve Personnel Selection and Enhance Human Capital: A Case Study in High-Technology Industry," *Expert Systems with Applications*, Vol. 34, No. 1, 2008.

[7] Ina S. Markham, "Assessing the Prediction of Employee Productivity: A Comparison of OLS vs. CART," *International Journal of Productivity and Quality Management*, Vol. 8, No. 3, 2011.

[8] Aaron Chalfin, Oren Danieli, Andrew Hillis, Zubin Jelveh, Michael Luca, Jens Ludwig, and Sendhil Mullainathan, "Productivity and Selection of Human Capital with Machine Learning," *American Economic Review*, Vol. 106, No. 5, 2016.

[9] Strohmeier and Piazza, 2013.

[10] Putka, Beatty, and Reeder, 2018.

and sensors have been used to measure and track new forms of biodata.[11] These developments are orthogonal to advances in ML. However, the number and diversity of potential predictor variables now available may necessitate using new approaches for ML.

Application of Prediction Methods to First-Term Enlistment Outcomes

We used a range of ML models to predict different outcomes for IST personnel based on a large set of predictor variables introduced in Chapter 3. This is informative with respect to the relative value of different and more advanced modeling techniques as well as the importance of including specific predictors in the models. The four outcomes we considered were (1) technical school training success, (2) promotion timing (whether an individual was promoted to E-5 during his or her first term), (3) first term completion, and (4) reenlistment. These outcomes go beyond simply predicting technical training success, which, although important, is generally high across USAF and does not address the range of considerations about future job outcomes.

All of these outcomes are represented as binary variables with a positive and negative value. Accordingly, the purpose of modeling these outcomes is to produce predicted probabilities for the positive outcomes (i.e., graduation, promotion, first-term completion, and reenlistment). For example, given a set of predictor variables for an individual, our models predict probabilities for each of these four outcomes. Given this framework, the task is to select predictor variables and models that maximize predictive performance.

Development of Machine Learning Models

Achieving high predictive performance requires selecting appropriate predictors for each outcome. Although ML models can automatically select appropriate predictors to some extent, their performance depends on the suitability and quality of predictor variables provided in the first place. Accordingly, we selected a limited set of predictor variables from the potentially vast set based on four criteria:

- **Availability:** By merging various different sources, we were able to utilize a wide range of predictors. Yet we remained restricted to the variables that existed in those databases.
- **Completeness:** We used only those predictors that contained enough completed records. Because we merged multiple data sources across partially overlapping subsets of individuals, many individuals were missing values for some variables. Predictors with high percentages of missing values were excluded due to both the limited information they provided and the practical challenges of accounting for missingness in the models.
- **Timing:** Variables were evaluated for appropriateness based on when they were collected relative to timing of the outcome of interest.

---

[11] Scott Tonidandel, Eden B. King, and Jose M. Cortina, "Big Data Methods: Leveraging Modern Data Analytic Techniques to Build Organizational Science," *Organizational Research Methods*, Vol. 21, No. 3, 2018.

- **Variability:** Certain variables that had nearly singular values for all individuals were excluded. Other variables were recoded to collapse many small categories into larger ones. This type of data cleaning, which aims to improve performance, interpretability, and computational speed, is standard practice.

An additional consideration is whether a variable or collection of variables may lead to unethical bias—for example, predicting outcomes based on protected categories like race, gender, and ethnicity. Guarding against algorithmic bias is important given the highly consequential nature of decisions (i.e., job assignments and career directions) that the predictive models may inform. All models were run with and without demographic variables to determine the magnitudes of their effects.

Table 4.2 summarizes all predictors considered for the corresponding outcomes. The table denotes variables currently used to assess probability of success in technical training—what we refer to as the *baseline model*.[12] This emulates the Job Spin model currently in use. The table also contains additional variables used in an *expanded model*. Some variables overlap, but with important differences. For example, in the baseline model, cognitive aptitude is measured at the level of ASVAB composite scores (from MAGE), whereas in the expanded model aptitude is measured at the level of subtest scores. Also, both models incorporate AFSC clusters to capture differences in outcomes for individuals in different AFSCs. The baseline model clusters AFSCs based on MAGE categories and whether or not an AFSC belongs to the special operations category. In contrast, the expanded model clusters AFSCs based on size and historical pass rates, as well as global career clusters, which are a more granular categorization than MAGE categories.

Table 4.2. Variables Used as Predictors and the Corresponding Outcome Variables

Predictor	Category	Baseline	Expanded
Age	Age at entry		X
AFQT category	Aptitude		X
MAGE score	Aptitude	X	
Arithmetic reasoning subtest (ASVAB)	Aptitude		X
Auto-shop information subtest (ASVAB)	Aptitude		X
Electrical information subtest (ASVAB)	Aptitude		X
Mechanical comprehension subtest (ASVAB)	Aptitude		X
Math knowledge subtest (ASVAB)	Aptitude		X
Paragraph comprehension subtest (ASVAB)	Aptitude		X
Word knowledge subtest (ASVAB)	Aptitude		X

---

[12] We were unable to perfectly replicate current baseline USAF selection and classification practices due to incomplete data on airman qualifications. Instead, we constructed a model that emulates the major elements of the baseline approach.

Predictor	Category	Baseline	Expanded
Global careers	AFSC clusters		X
Class size cluster	AFSC clusters		X
Outcome rate	AFSC clusters		X
MAGE category	AFSC cluster	X	
Special ops AFSC	AFSC cluster	X	
Ethnicity[a]	Demographics		X
Gender[a]	Demographics		X
Marital status[a]	Demographics		X
Dependents[a]	Demographics		X
Race[a]	Demographics		X
Religion[a]	Demographics		X
Academic	Education level		X
Bonus	Enlistment factors		X
Term of enlistment[b]	Enlistment factors	X	X
Entry pay grade[b]	Enlistment factors		X
First language	First language		X
Algebra	High school courses	X	X
Biology	High school courses	X	X
Chemistry	High school courses	X	X
English	High school courses	X	X
Geometry	High school courses	X	X
Physics	High school courses	X	X
Trigonometry	High school courses	X	X
Typing	High school courses	X	X
Height	Medical/Physical		X
Weight	Medical/Physical		X
PULHES E	Medical/Physical	X	X
PULHES L	Medical/Physical	X	X
Strength Aptitude Test (SAT)	Medical/Physical	X	X
1st preference	Preferences	X	X
2nd preference	Preferences	X	X
3rd preference	Preferences	X	X
4th preference	Preferences	X	X
Junior Reserve Officers' Training Corps (JROTC) category	Service experience	X	X
Peace Corps	Service experience	X	X
Waiver category	Waiver		X
Waiver status	Waiver		X

[a] Variables that should be excluded due to concern of unethical bias.
[b] Excluded from prediction of training success.

We compared prediction accuracy for different ML approaches applied to baseline and expanded variable sets. For the baseline variable set, we explored only logistic regression in a GLM to best emulate the current practice. For the expanded variable set, we evaluated logistic regression, lasso regression, RF, and BART.[13] Thus, we evaluated a total of five models: baseline GLM, expanded GLM, expanded Lasso, expanded RF, and expanded BART.

Evaluation of Machine Learning Models

The models' output predicted probabilities for each outcome and individual. These outputs are "true" predictions in that the models are trained using only a subset of historical data and then tested on held-out cases that were not used to train the models.[14] We evaluated these outputs and the associated models in two ways:

1. **Classification error:** This is the most common metric used to evaluate model performance due to its intuitive meaning and practical importance. It describes the number of correct classifications divided by the total number of cases. Predicted probabilities above 0.5 are treated as positive outcomes, and probabilities below 0.5 are treated as negative outcomes. Model outcomes are then compared with true outcomes to determine the percentages that match. If the two classes of outcomes are highly imbalanced, classification error can be misleading because a model that simply predicts the more likely class will perform reasonably well. This is shown to be the case for technical training outcomes, where the overall passing rate is 90.8 percent.

2. **Receiver operating characteristic (ROC) curves with their corresponding area under the curve (AUC):** AUC describes the probability that the classifier will rank a randomly chosen positive example (i.e., an individual eliminated from his or her first technical training pipeline) more highly than a negative example. AUC helps to evaluate the models when outcome classes are highly imbalanced because they consider the entire distribution of predicted probabilities rather than simply counting how many values fall above or below 0.5. ROC creates a visualization of performance and AUC summarizes performance as a single value. The value of AUC is used for relative comparison, and it ranges from 0.5 to 1, with 0.5 denoting chance prediction and 1.0 denoting perfect prediction.

Table 4.3 shows predictive performance metrics for the four outcomes and three models. For comparison, we show the baseline GLM, expanded GLM, and the best performing ML model. All model results are given in Appendix B. When we applied GLM to the baseline and then used expanded variable sets, the predictive performance of all four outcomes increased. This is reflected in the decreased classification error and increased AUC. Applying more advanced

---

[13] We considered other methods in Table 4.1, but ultimately excluded them because they did not increase predictive performance and they had lower interpretability than other methods used.

[14] Models were trained using four partitions of the complete data and they were tested on the fifth, withheld partition (i.e., fivefold cross-validation).

ML models to the expanded variable set produced additional, but modest, gains in predictive performance. On the whole, these results show that expanding the set of predictor variables may substantially improve predictive outcomes and adopting more advanced ML models may provide relatively small gains in utility (but can be more computationally costly). The results also show that given the relatively low variability in technical training outcomes, the models may have the most utility when predicting other first-term outcomes.

Table 4.3. Improvement in Classification Accuracy over the Baseline Model

Outcome	Method	Percentage Classification Error	AUC
Graduate technical training	Baseline GLM	7.03	0.761
	Expanded GLM	7.05	0.861
	BART (best ML model)	6.96	0.873
Promotion to E-5 after first term	Baseline GLM	32.36	0.717
	Expanded GLM	27.23	0.788
	BART (best ML model)	25.79	0.813
Reenlistment	Baseline GLM	42.26	0.590
	Expanded GLM[a]	38.57	0.672
	BART (best ML model)	36.92	0.694
Early separation	Baseline GLM	25.35	0.635
	Expanded GLM	20.78	0.738
	BART (best ML model)	20.08	0.750

[a] GLM did not converge for reenlistment model. Results show GLM with Lasso regularization.

Determining Which Variables Matter the Most

Having determined that the largest increase in predictive performance comes from including additional variables, we next turned to evaluating the relative importance among those variables. Of the ML approaches that we used, RFs produce estimates of relative importance based on the contribution of each variable to the overall accuracy of the predictions. In other words, importance is measured by how much the prediction would worsen if the model did not include a given variable.

Figure 4.2 shows the relative importance for groupings of variables with respect to predicting each of the four outcomes. Importance is categorized into four levels from low to high. Cells in dark red denote high importance of the variable group for the corresponding outcome measure, whereas cells in light pink denote low importance. AFSC differences (i.e., clusters),[15] aptitude (i.e., ASVAB scores), and education level are consistently the most important groups of

---

[15] See Chapter 3 for a description of these clusters.

Figure 4.2. Heatmap of Relative Importance of Variable Groupings for Four Outcomes

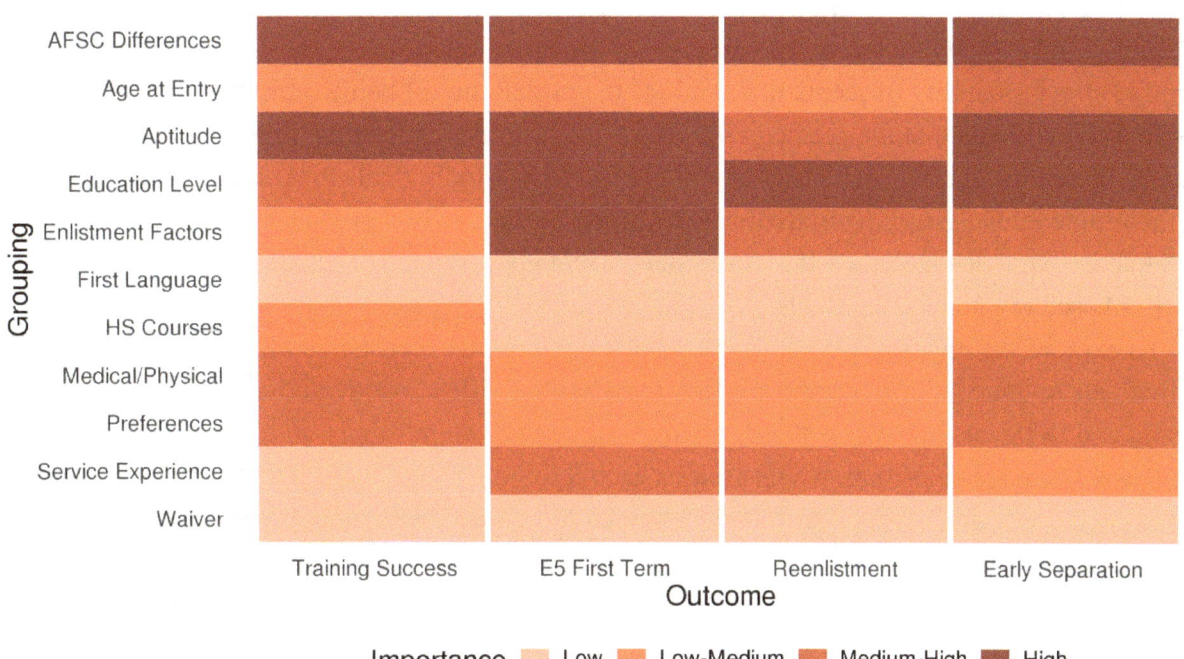

predictors. Other groups such as enlistment factors, preferences, service experience, medical/ physical, and age are of medium to high importance for some but not all outcomes. Finally, variables such as first language, high school courses, and waivers are of low importance for all outcomes.

These results demonstrate the benefits of using more granular measures than those already included in the baseline model.[16] For example, using ASVAB subset scores rather than MAGE composites may improve prediction. Additionally, these results demonstrate the benefits of including new measures. For example, educational attainment is an important predictor for all outcomes and is already routinely obtained. Finally, these results demonstrate that the benefits of including certain measures, such as medical/physical status, are limited to a subset of outcomes.

---

[16] Due to the large volume of missing TAPAS data described in Chapter 3, we did not include TAPAS in the full model evaluations. However, we conducted similar analyses using the data that was available for TAPAS to evaluate the potential benefits that could be gained by inclusion in the prediction models. The results of these analyses indicated that TAPAS provided only marginal improvements in prediction accuracy. Despite the limited contribution to prediction accuracy in these analyses, future analyses may find value in predicting success for specific AFSCs. Our analyses, which model outcomes across AFSC clusters, may mask some important nuances at the AFSC level. Additional analyses will also be needed as TAPAS undergoes further modifications and improvements.

Application of Model Outcomes to Job Assignment

The ML models we evaluated predict four outcomes for each individual per AFS: (1) the probability of completing technical training; (2) the probability of completing the first enlisted term; (3) the probability of reenlisting; and (4) the probability of being promoted to E-5 during the first term. Given that the predictor variables used are available at the time of enlistment or shortly thereafter, the ML models could be used to assign individuals to AFSs to maximize any of these outcomes. Assigning individuals to career fields based on predicted outcomes of the baseline or expanded models differs from the current approach, in which airmen are assigned to AFSCs based on qualifications, class start dates, and stated preferences (see Chapter 2).

To explore the implications of this alternate approach, we considered all non-GTEP individuals assigned to jobs during the first month of FY 2019. We treated individuals as the *supply* and IST seats by AFS as the *demand*. To optimally align supply and demand, we used the Kuhn-Munkres algorithm, which assigns each individual to a unique IST seat to maximize the objective function. For example, the expanded ML model predicts the probabilities that an individual will complete technical training for all possible AFSs. The optimization routine can maximize the summed probabilities of completing technical training across all non-GTEP individuals.

Figure 4.3 (top left) shows the results of using the optimization routine in this way. Each point in the plot is an individual. Placement along the x-axis is the predicted probability that the individual will complete technical training for their actual AFS, and placement along the y-axis is the predicted probability that the individual will complete technical training given optimized assignment. The diagonal line indicates the same predicted probability for the actual and optimized assignment.

As the clustering of yellow dots on and above the diagonal line in the figure shows, optimized assignment slightly increases the predicted pass rate for most individuals. The predicted cumulative pass rate between the actual AFS and the optimized assignment increases by about 2 percent. On the one hand, these figures shows that individuals are already assigned to suitable technical training pipelines. On the other hand, some individuals would benefit greatly from a different assignment. This is the case for the highlighted individual (shown by the red arrow). Moving Airman Brown from an AFS with a low pass rate to one with a high pass rate greatly increases the probability of completing technical training. This creates a vacancy in Airman Brown's original AFS that must be filled. Moving Airman Smith from an AFS with a high pass rate to the one with a low pass rate slightly decreases the probability of completing technical training, but to a far lesser extent than for Airman Brown.

Figure 4.3 also shows the results of applying the optimization routine to each outcome measure. As compared with completing technical training, placing an individual in the optimal pipeline resulted in larger gains on the order of 5 percent to 7 percent for job performance (completing the first term and promotion) and reenlistment. This indicates that adopting a more expansive view that encompasses first-term and career outcomes can help USAF match airmen to AFSs to achieve a variety of important organizational outcomes.

Figure 4.3. Results of Applying Optimization Routine to Each Outcome Measure

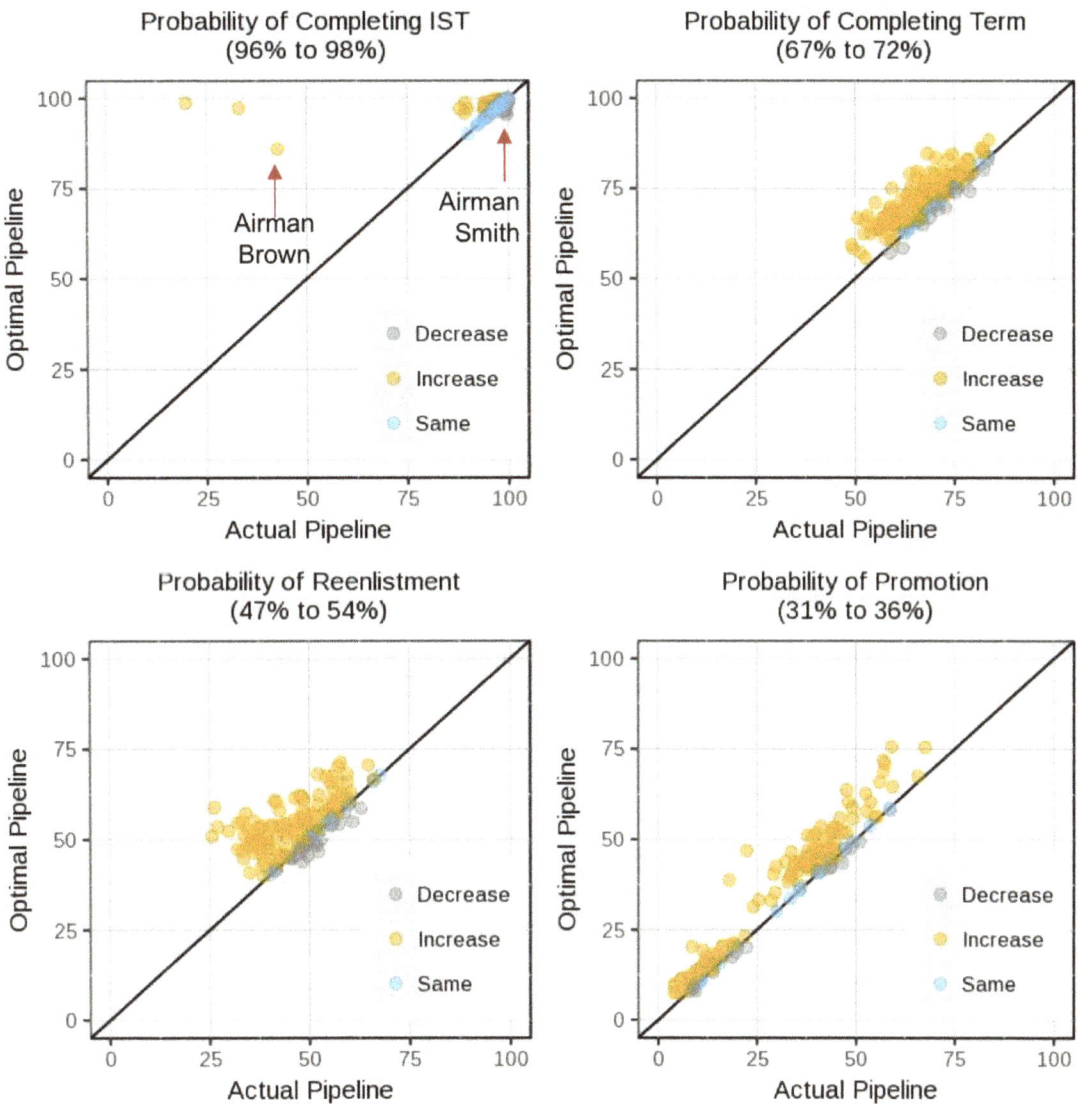

NOTE: Values in parentheses show expected changes in outcome probabilities for optimized assignments versus standard assignments.

A limitation of the approach as described is that it focuses on each outcome at the expense of the others. The results shown in the separate panels of Figure 4.3 reflect totally different AFSC assignments, assignments that may adversely affect the other outcomes not used for optimization. To deal with this limitation, we ran the optimization routine on a composite that combined information across the four outcomes, weighted according to their notional importance. We considered two cases—one with equal weight assigned to each outcome (*balanced composite*) and another with greatest weight assigned to completing technical training (*tech composite*).[17]

---

[17] *Tech Composite = 1.5 × CompleteTech + 1.0 × CompleteTerm + 0.2 × Reenlist + 0.1 × ReachE5*

Table 4.4 shows results based on optimizing each outcome separately versus optimizing the composite. Optimizing each outcome separately produced the best result per outcome but at the expense of the others. Conversely, optimizing based on the composites produces very good results for all outcomes, results that exceed the outcomes expected given actual AFS assignments. The expected probabilities of completing the first term, of reenlisting, and of reaching E-5 during the first term increased by 3 percent, 5 percent, and 3 percent, respectively. This suggests that all outcomes should be considered when determining the optimal AFS assignments.

Table 4.4. Outcome Based on Optimizing Single Measures Versus Composite Measure

Optimized Outcome	Outcome Measure as Percentage			
	Complete Technical Training	Complete First Term	Reenlist	Reach E-5
Complete technical training	98	67	47	32
Complete first term	94	72	48	32
Reenlist	94	67	54	33
Reach E-5	94	67	48	36
Balanced composite	96	70	52	34
Tech composite	97	70	50	33
Baseline	96	67	47	31

A tacit assumption in this analysis is that airmen are willing to accept the optimized assignments. The benefits of this approach would be undermined, however, if, for instance, airmen had little interest in their assigned career fields. Such preferences could be provided to the optimization routine to increase the probabilities of positive technical training and career outcomes.

Summary

Our application of ML to USAF personnel data for purposes of predicting technical training success, job performance, and reenlistment outcomes revealed four findings. First, expanding the set of predictor variables to include more diverse and granular measures improved prediction performance. Second, leveraging more complex ML techniques produced additional, albeit small, gains in prediction performance. Third, benefits were greatest when predicting job performance and reenlistment outcomes, which, unlike technical training success, were not uniformly high. Collectively, these three findings demonstrate that the benefits of the ML techniques are greatest when outcomes are relatively balanced (i.e., hard to predict) and when a large set of predictor variables are provided. Fourth, by optimizing assignment of individuals to jobs based on a composite index, job performance and retention outcomes can be improved while maintaining— or slightly improving—technical training outcomes.

5. Optimization Model for Reclassifying Training Eliminations

In this chapter, we analyze approaches to reclassifying enlisted airmen who are eliminated during IST to evaluate potential cost savings and improvements in training outcomes. For this analysis, we present a mathematical optimization model for computing the costs and outcomes of different trainee reclassifications among USAF enlisted specialties during IST. Using data from 2018 IST eliminations, we developed a model to estimate the potential benefits of a structured reclassification method. This model provides an exploration of a recommender system for IST reclassifications for individual airmen;[1] it should therefore be used to consider the value of new approaches to IST reclassifications and the utility of developing a more dynamic algorithm for guiding real-time reclassification decisions.[2]

Background

Reclassification is an important part of the IST process and has a notable impact on USAF costs and on the fulfillment of manpower requirements. Managing reclassifications, however, is not an insignificant challenge; the number of trainees reclassified into different USAF enlisted specialties during IST has steadily increased in recent years with FY 2018 being an exception (see Chapter 1). However, as described in Chapter 2, reclassification to a new specialty is performed manually and tends to be ad hoc and performed just in time because both the elimination of trainees and the availability of open seats are uncertain and dynamic. The benefits of improved placement of airmen or better administrative processes for placing them can be examined through modeling.

The reclassification determination differs from the original classification and IST assignment, which is handled by the JobSpin/CareerSpin models.[3] During BMT, these models calculate a score for each airman for each available IST training seat. Next, for each airman, the model

---

[1] A recommender or recommendation system is an information system that predicts or suggests an item that meets the user's observed preferences without making the selection (e.g., online movie streaming services may suggest additional content the user may like).

[2] The model we examine reclassifies an annual cohort of airmen simultaneously to satisfy overall goals for USAF. It is a one-period model with no explicit dependence on past reclassification decisions for any individual in the cohort. In actuality, reclassification decisions for individuals are executed frequently throughout the year. Reclassifying individuals as soon as the need for reclassification becomes apparent in real time requires a "dynamic" model to ensure that the sequence of past individual reclassification decisions over the course of the year would satisfy the same overall goals for USAF as the one-period model does.

[3] Sparkman, 2010. Additionally, this is partially based on the descriptions contained in an internal USAF document of a prototype called "Career Spin." The document was provided to the RAND project team by AETC's Study and Analysis Squadron in August 2018.

assigns the IST course training seat that maximizes the aggregate sum of scores across all airmen within intervals of weeks. The model assigns each airman to exactly one IST course seat and is constrained by the number of training seats available.

Uncertainty and dynamism in course availability and training eliminations create challenges for the development of similarly structured reclassification models that can be used in real-time. These models are designed for use for one time period and are actionable only when used with a planning horizon of several months to a year. However, coupled with retrospective analyses of past reclassifications, such models can still establish bounds on the expected costs and benefits of reclassifying an eliminated cohort differently.

To evaluate alternate approaches to reclassification, we developed a one-period reclassification model inspired by Job Spin/Career Spin using retrospective data from 2018 reclassifications. We then used this model to conduct additional analyses that examine the following two objectives:

1. reclassification of airmen into an AFSC in a way that minimizes costs, ensures sufficient training outcomes, and satisfies USAF requirements; additionally, discussion of trade-offs among these objectives that can inform the potential value of developing more dynamic reclassification algorithms in the future
2. accounting of average costs and delay of having an airman wait for entry to an IST course for a particular specialty; additionally, examination of the consequences of a manual reclassifier using a particular look-ahead period (i.e., reclassify airman within two weeks versus one week, and so on).

Methodology

Although the reclassification model used for the analysis is a mathematical optimization model inspired by Job Spin/Career Spin, it does feature notable differences. Foremost, the aim of the analysis is to demonstrate whether reduced costs or improved training outcomes are possible by assigning the approximately 1,700 reclassified airmen in 2018 to AFSCs that are different from their initial reclassifications. The intent is not to provide an actual reclassification algorithm, but to demonstrate the potential benefits of a better reclassification. Although the model accounts for average time for a training seat to become available, it does not account for the actual times for each training seat by AFSC. For example, the model does consider that a course of initial entry for an AFSC is available every 15 days on average, but does not consider more granular real-time information such as whether it is possible to assign an airman needing classification on January 1 and assignment to an available course seat by January 16. This level of detail would be required for an implementable, real-time reclassification algorithm.

Model Description

The optimization model is designed to find an AFSC assignment for each individual airman that minimizes total cost, ensures sufficient outcomes, and respects USAF training requirements. We consider two primary elements for costs of reclassifying an individual airman: (1) the average imputed cost of waiting for a suitable IST course, which we refer to as the cost of "idling" the airman; and (2) the cost of relocating the airman near the course training location associated with the prospective AFSC. Previous training costs and past pay are not factored as they are sunk costs.[4]

We consider four possible training and career outcomes associated with an individual airman's assignment to a particular AFSC. These outcomes are calculated as probabilities, or likelihoods, based on data-driven predictions (see Chapter 4 for details). Specifically, we consider likelihoods of the following outcomes: (1) successfully graduating from IST for the first assigned AFSC (*training success*); (2) separating before the first enlistment term is completed (*early separation*); (3) being promoted to E-5 in the first enlistment term (*promotion*); and (4) reenlistment after the first term (*reenlistment*). Moreover, we consider a combined training and career outcome, which we refer to as a *grand success*, as the joint likelihood of an individual airman completing training, not separating early, reenlisting, and being promoted as a result of being assigned to a specific AFSC. The likelihood of a "grand success is the product of the likelihoods of promotion, reenlistment, and not separating early (i.e., 1 minus the likelihood of early separation) and is inclusive of training success.

The model enforces several constraints and requires that AFSC assignment for individual airmen respect the following:

- each airman is reclassified to exactly one AFSC
- the total number of assignments to an AFSC does not exceed USAF training requirements for that AFSC
- airmen are not reclassified to an AFSC from which they were eliminated
- the overall assignment produces a sufficient number of positive training and career outcomes.

An alternative variant of the model maximizes the number of positive training and career outcomes within a given budget for idle and relocation costs. Appendix C presents the optimization model formulation.

Data and Assumptions

We obtained the necessary data for the model from various sources. Unless specified otherwise, all data are for FY 2018.

---

[4] Additional costs associated with reclassification, such as labor costs for personnel processing reclassification packages and unobserved costs from unfilled training seats, are also not part of our model. Instead, we analyze potential costs that are directly considered by those who are making reclassification decisions.

Costs

Costs were decomposed into estimates of idle and relocation costs and were specific for each airman-AFSC combination. Idle costs represent the average cost of waiting for the entry IST course for an AFSC. These were estimated using actual FY 2018 IST course schedules. Dynamic, real-time reclassification algorithms will need to make use of exact course dates instead of relying on the average waiting time for the course to be available. We assumed the daily cost for an "idle" airman, inclusive of pay, housing, and tax collected through the Federal Insurance Contributions Act (FICA) to be $110 per day.[5]

Relocation costs depend on the airman's current location and the specific AFSC he or she is reclassified into. For each airman, we begin with the training base of the IST he or she was eliminated from and then identify the new training base/course training location if the airman was reclassified into a particular AFSC. Once the likely origin-destination pairs were calculated, we estimated the relocation costs using the U.S. General Services Administration transportation and relocation rates per mile.[6]

Requirements

The model enforces that the total number assignments into an AFSC do not exceed training requirements. These data were computed from the FY 2018 Enlisted Initial Skills (EIS) Program Guidance Letter (PGL),[7] which establishes priorities and identifies which AFSCs can produce up to 20 percent, 10 percent, or 0 percent over the EIS PGL amount. We calculated the maximum number of reclassifications each AFSC would allow from this data.[8]

Outcomes

The various training and career outcomes and their likelihoods for each airman-AFSC combination were estimated using the RF methods detailed in Chapter 4. Using the individual characteristics from that implementation, the predicted probabilities of each outcome for every potential AFSC were included in the optimization model as described in Appendix C. These estimates are airman-specific and predictive in nature.

---

[5] FICA is the payroll tax deducted from U.S. employee paychecks. We estimate approximately $110 per day and airman based on an annual estimate of $40K per airmen.

[6] U.S. General Services Administration, "Privately Owned Vehicle (POV) Mileage Reimbursement Rates," webpage, September 13, 2019. We assumed the most expensive rates of $1.26 per mile (airplane) and relocation rate of $0.20 per mile. Approximate distances between origin-destination pairs were calculated using geographic coordinates and the spherical law of cosines.

[7] EIS refers to the "the total validated enlisted technical training requirements necessary for force sustainment in each Air Force Specialty Code." See U.S. Air Force Manual 36-2100, p. 109. The PGL is used by AETC "to develop course schedules that will meet the requirements" (Harrington et al., 2017, p. 1).

[8] We allowed each AFSC to be able to accept at least one reclassification.

Policy Simulation

We used the aforementioned data to examine the possibility and surrounding trade-offs of having the model reclassify all airmen who were reclassified in FY 2018. This policy simulation compares the model-based reclassification with reclassification that occurred in actuality. We compared the costs and outcomes of the model-based reclassification with the actual reclassification that occurred. Moreover, we use the model to show the consequences of a manual reclassifier using a particular look-ahead period (i.e., reclassify airman within two weeks versus one week, and so on) when performing the reclassifications ad-hoc.

Study Population

For this analysis, we focused on all airmen who were reclassified exactly once in 2018 ($N = 1,732$) and were also reclassified into/from 123 AFSCs for which we were able to predict training and career outcomes ($n = 1,544$).

Simulation Baseline

Using the model and data on the actual reclassification that occurred for the study population, we computed the predicted costs and outcomes. These serve as the baseline for all the results. We also added additional constraints to the optimization model so that the obtained model-based reclassification matched or exceeded the positive training outcomes predicted for the baseline or had a lower total cost than the baseline.

Analysis of Look-Ahead Periods and Scenarios Used in the Simulation

We compare the actual reclassification that occurred for the study population with the model-based reclassification for six different scenarios. These scenarios vary by either the objective (minimizing cost or maximizing grand success) or the length of the look-ahead period (infinite, one week, two weeks, three weeks, and four weeks). As stated above, USAF is currently performing the reclassifications manually and ad-hoc based on immediate availability of IST course seats at the time of reclassification. A consequence of this is that the reclassifier may be using a short-term look-ahead (i.e., forcing reclassification within one or two weeks ahead to find the best AFSC for the airman) and possibly reclassifying airmen prematurely. For example, it might be worthwhile to consider a more formal or longer look-ahead policy whereby USAF is potentially better served by allowing airmen to idle longer so that they are assigned to a better AFSC. Figure 5.1 shows that on average, 80 percent of AFSCs allowing entry in FY 2018 were available for course entry within approximately 35 days. Provided course capacity is sufficient, this raises the possibility that moving away from immediate reclassification could be compensated for by obtaining an AFSC assignment with better training outcomes. The one-period

Figure 5.1. Histogram of Average Days Between Successive Initial Skills Training Entry Course Start Dates Across Air Force Specialties (Fiscal Year 2018)

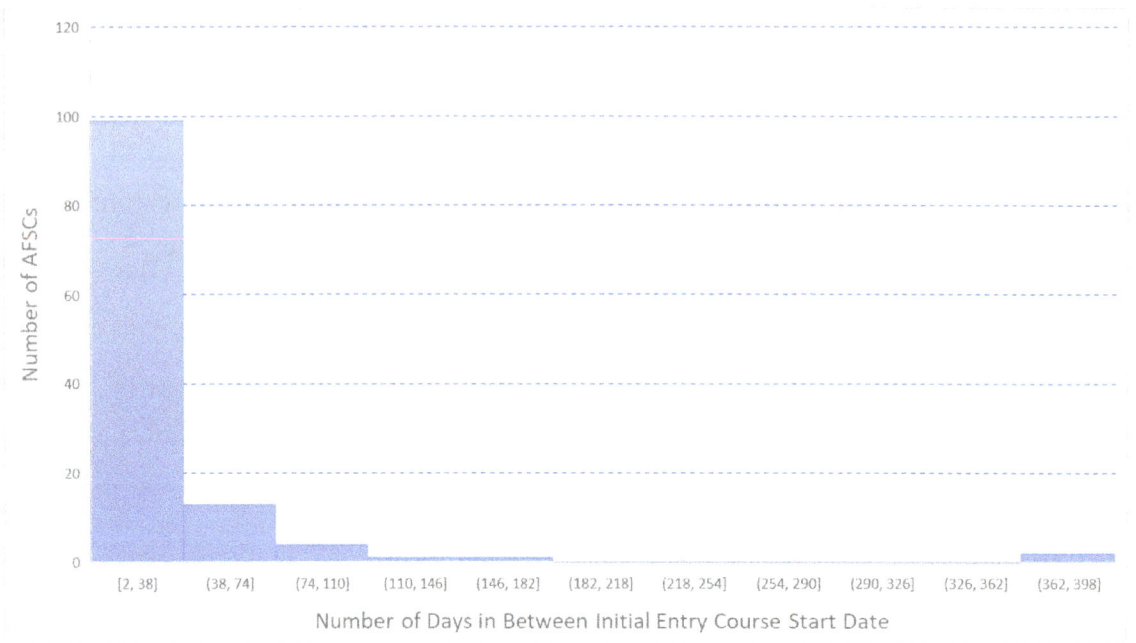

NOTE: Numbers on the horizontal axis are ranges of days grouping AFSs by number of days between successive IST entry course start dates. For example, 2–38 days is the range of days between successive IST entry course start dates for approximately 100 AFSs.

optimization model described above and in Appendix C was used to reclassify airmen in all six scenarios.[9]

Results

Figures 5.2 and 5.3 show the differences between the model results, which minimize cost over an infinite planning horizon as described in more detail in Appendix C, and the historical

---

[9] Unlike the dynamic reclassifications that USAF in fact performs, the one-period optimization model described in Appendix C has the advantage of reclassifying a single-year cohort simultaneously and allowing for both finite and infinite look-ahead periods. This allows us to obtain bounds on how much USAF could improve cost or training outcomes by pursuing different reclassification methods, as the benefits from a dynamic model would be bounded by the benefits of a one-period model with infinite look-ahead. There is a technical explanation for this. Analytically, given a look-ahead period of K weeks (i.e., forcing reclassification of all airmen within K weeks on average), for a specific airman-AFSC combination, we can set the idle costs to $M \gg 0$ if the frequency of the IST course to enter that AFSC is less than once every K weeks (i.e., the model assigns unreasonably high cost from assigning an airman to an infrequently offered AFSC). This is widely known as the "Big M" technique in operations research. We then re-solve the optimization model. If we obtain an optimal cost with the same order of magnitude as M or larger, then we know it was impossible to assign each airman to an AFSC within K weeks on average. We continue this until we find the smallest such K with a reasonable optimal cost (K^*). This value is the minimum amount of time, on average, for which the manual reclassifier can find a new AFSC for all the airmen needing reclassification. We can then compare the results of the model with a look-ahead of K^* versus the original model to determine whether adopting K^* is a reasonable policy for the manual reclassifier and how much USAF potentially loses (relative to the infinite look-ahead model) by being myopic in this regard.

outcomes for individual reclassifications. The histograms in Figure 5.2 represent the distribution of probability spreads (difference between the model-selected ISTs and historical ISTs) of training success, early separation, reenlistment, and promotion. The greater the value from zero, the higher the improvement likelihood of each positive outcome. Within Figure 5.2, the distributions for training success, early separation, reenlistment, and promotion are all centered on zero. The distribution of differences in the probability of grand success for the model and historical assignments, shown in Figure 5.3, are also centered on zero. The figures therefore

Figure 5.2. Histograms of Differences Between Model-Driven Outcomes

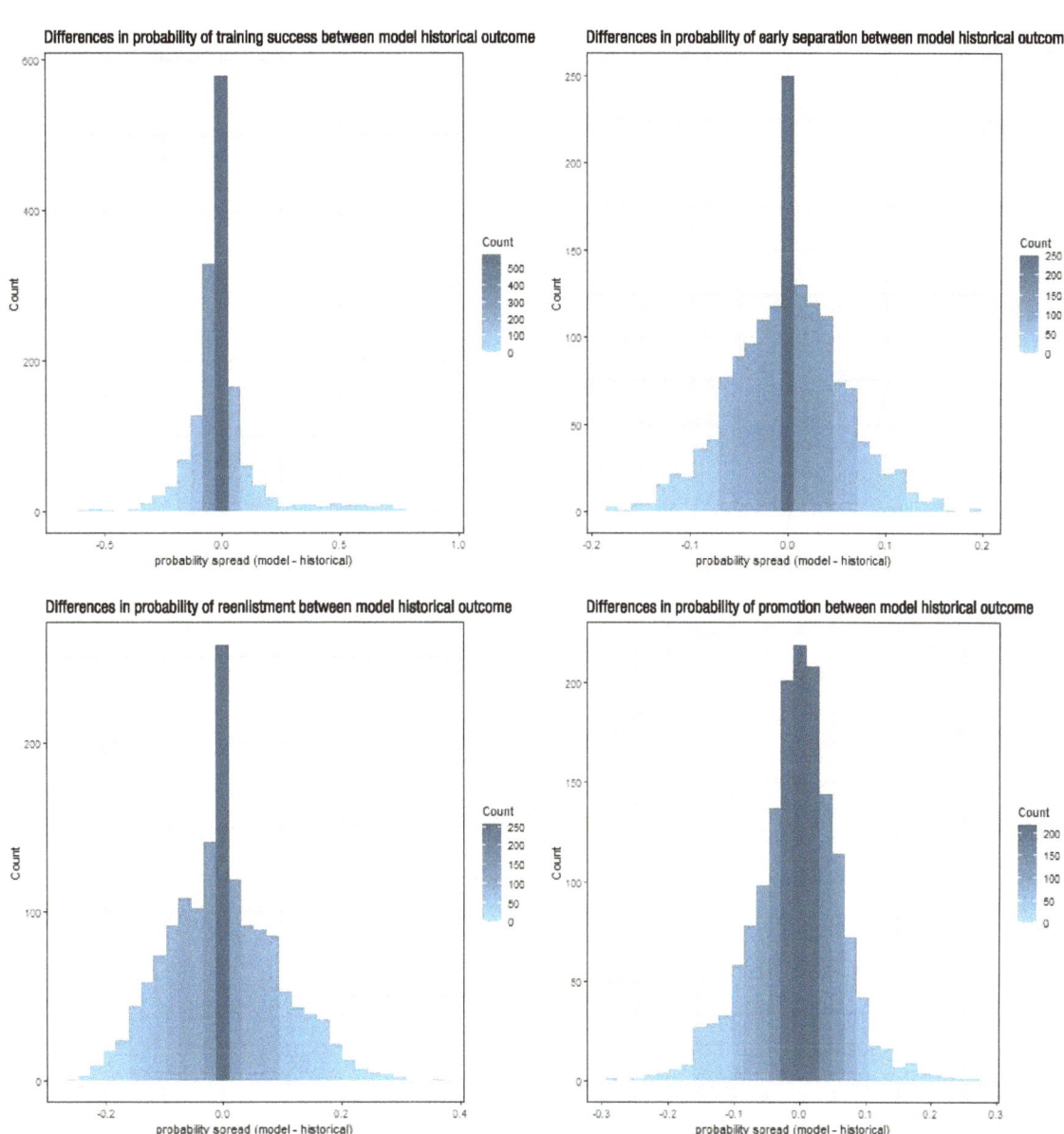

NOTE: This figure depicts the difference between model reclassifications and historical assignments through four histograms. Each histogram shows the distribution of differences between model and historical probabilities of training success (upper left), early separation (upper right), reenlistment (lower left), and promotion (lower right). Lighter colors represent greater frequencies.

45

Figure 5.3. Histogram of Difference Between Model and Historical Probabilities of Grand Success

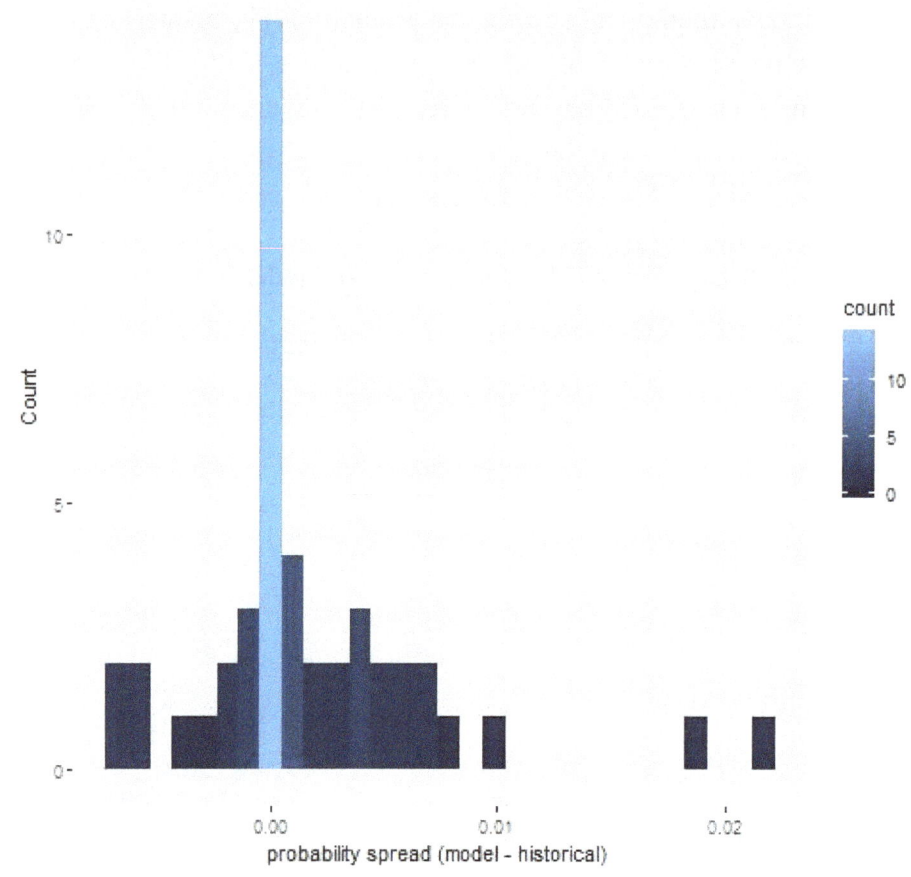

NOTE: This figure depicts the distribution of differences between model and historical probabilities of grand success. Lighter colors represent larger frequencies.

confirm that the model is performing similar to the baseline, a constraint imposed in the optimization problem. That is, each histogram essentially confirms that the model performs as intended, on average, with some deviations for individual airmen.

The overall results of the analysis are shown in Table 5.1. We compare the results of the optimization model in different scenarios with one-, two-, three-, and four-week look-aheads and with an infinite look-ahead. Comparing each outcome in terms of estimated cost, early separations, promotions, training successes, and grand successes, we find room for overall improvement from the baseline in all scenarios. In all scenarios, the model generates a lower total cost than the baseline. Gains in grand success are achieved in each scenario, particularly the scenario where the number of grand successes is the objective to be maximized. Moreover, the different scenarios did not significantly affect the total number of training successes, which is a limiting factor when either cost or grand successes are optimized. We also find that most gains are achieved within a two- to four-week time horizon and that a four-week look-ahead minimizing cost can lead to improved outcomes.

Table 5.1. Summary of Model Results

Scenario	Model Objective	Estimated Total Cost	Estimated Idle Costs (at $110 per day)	Estimated Idle Days	Estimated Relocation Costs	Early Separations	Promotions	Reenlistments	Training Successes	Grand Successes
Baseline	—	$8,873,165	$7,682,514	69,841	$1,190,651	441.97	574.45	718.88	1,368.26	197.29
Infinite look-ahead[a]	Cost	$1,693,189	$1,328,336	12,076	$364,853	441.96	574.62	718.89	1,368.33	199.32
Infinite look-ahead[b]	Grand successes	$4,375,387	$3,321,437	30,195	$1,053,949	403.50	645.56	781.11	1368.31	252.07
1-week look-ahead[c]	Cost	N/A	N/A	N/A	N/A	N/A	N/A	N/A	N/A	N/A
2-week look-ahead[c]	Cost	$1,736,354	$1,276,789	11,607	$459,565	441.97	574.48	718.92	1,368.35	198.91
3-week look-ahead[c]	Cost	$1,695,802	$1,308,954	11,900	$386,848	441.94	574.53	718.88	1,368.34	199.36
4-week look-ahead[c]	Cost	$1,693,189	$1,328,336	12,076	$364,853	441.96	574.62	718.89	1,368.33	199.32

NOTES: N = 1,544. One-week look-ahead did not produce a solution within a feasible cost; the implication is that USAF will not be able to assign everyone to an IST in one week, on average (instead it takes at least two weeks to assign everyone on average).

[a] Constrained to match or exceed the baseline scenario's outcomes.
[b] Constrained to match or exceed the baseline scenario's cost.
[c] Constrained to match or exceed baseline scenario outcomes.

47

Summary

The mathematical optimization model introduced in this chapter explores the potential value of a recommender system for IST reclassification. While the optimization model is not intended to be directly implemented by USAF for actual IST reclassifications, it provides potential improvements in IST reclassifications that can be gained through enhanced optimization. As a result, we find merit in further development of a more dynamic algorithm for guiding real-time USAF reclassification decisions. This merit arises from the potential gains in terms of both cost and positive career outcomes.

Our findings reveal that USAF might not be using the minimal cost solution for IST reclassification or the reclassification procedure that produces the maximum number of positive training and career outcomes. While there is a trade-off between cost and positive outcomes, improvements are feasible. For example, alternative reclassifications that match or exceed the outcomes associated with actual reclassifications might be possible at a lower cost. Similarly, alternative reclassifications that match cost associated with the actual reclassification might produce superior training and career outcomes. This trade-off between cost and positive outcomes could be overcome by a shift in policy; by removing the focus on immediate training successes, USAF may be able to achieve improved outcomes in both directions.[10]

Furthermore, the optimization model sheds light on optimal timing of airmen reclassifications. We find that USAF will be unlikely to optimally reclassify all airmen within one week on average. However, USAF can reclassify all airmen within two to four weeks on average and should be able to receive the highest marginal benefit through a four-week decision time frame. In a similar light, we additionally find that USAF may be "idling" airmen needing reclassification for more time than is necessary and that gains could come from shorter waiting periods.

Finally, we see the potential for improvements in reclassification in terms of better costs and outcomes. While we find that improvements could be achieved by computing the optimization model dynamically, both the computation and the real-time implementing of its solution would require further research and development. However, the optimization model constructed in this chapter is capable of calculating bounds on the potential benefits of such an effort pointing to potential gains. We estimate significant possible reduction in idle time and thereby cost. Additionally, we predict up to 55 more grand successes from better FY 2018 reclassifications.

Our exploration of an optimization-based IST reclassification recommender system suggests that USAF could realize potential gains from such an approach compared with the current approach to making reclassification decisions. Within current policies, an algorithm-based system can reduce costs or improve immediate training and long-term career outcomes. However, through further development and potential shifts in policy, gains in both cost reductions and positive outcomes appear possible.

---

[10] This result follows from the fact that training success is a binding constraint in both cost- and grand-success optimization.

6. Airmen Experiences in Initial Skills Training for Select Specialties

In this chapter, we review findings from focus groups designed to help us take a deeper dive into select specialties by exploring airmen's experiences with AFS selection and knowledge of AFSs prior to IST as well as how experiences in IST may tie to IST outcomes (e.g., graduation, reclassification). In conducting this deeper dive, we focused on nine specialties across the following occupational categories:

- Aerospace Medical Service (4N0X1)
- Air Traffic Control (1C1X1)
- Career Enlisted Aviation: Airborne Mission Systems (1A3X1), Aircraft Loadmaster (1A2X1), Special Missions Aviation (1A9X1)
- Cyber: Client Systems (3D1X1), Cyber Systems Operations (3D0X2), Cyber Transport Systems (3D1X2)
- Security Forces (3P0X1).

We selected these specialties because they had either above-average reclassification rates or large numbers of reclassified airmen in recent years. We considered other factors as well to make the final selection (see Appendix D).

Focus Group Approach

To gather information on airmen's knowledge and experiences within each of these specialties, we conducted 28 exploratory focus groups with a total of 165 airmen currently in IST. Table 6.1 shows the total number of focus groups and participants per specialty. Participants were active-duty, NPS airmen who had completed at least several blocks of their technical training, with the goal that airmen had enough training experience to comment on challenges they may have faced or were facing in completing IST.[1] The exact point in the training pipeline for each AFS was determined in consultation with the training pipeline managers. Appendix D provides an overview of focus group participant demographics.

Consistent with the purpose of many qualitative research methods, the use of focus groups allowed us the opportunity to ask open-ended questions designed to gather rich qualitative

---

[1] Seven airmen who participated in the focus groups were either prior-service or Air National Guard or Reserve members. Given that they would have different knowledge and experiences with AFS selection, we did not include their comments in that part of the analysis. We did include their comments as part of the analysis exploring experiences within IST.

Table 6.1. Number of Focus Groups and Participants by Specialty

Specialty	Group Code	Number of Focus Groups	Number of Participants
Aerospace Medical Service	4N0X1	4	23
Air Traffic Control (ATC)	1C1X1	4	23
Airborne Mission System	1A3X1	3	16
Loadmaster	1A2X1	4	22
Special Mission Aviation	1A9X1	2	9
Client Systems/Cyber Systems Operation[a]	3D1X1/3D0X2	4	27
Cyber Transport Systems	3D1X2	4	28
Security Forces	3P0X1	3	17

[a] Students from these cyber specialties were combined in our focus groups due to training schedule constraints.

information regarding airmen's knowledge and experiences when joining USAF and during IST.[2] Questions focused on two broad areas: (1) the information airmen received on potential careers or specialties before technical training and whether they had received their preferred specialty; and (2) experiences in technical training, including perceived factors that contribute to success versus reasons students struggle, washback, or washout. We also asked airmen what preparation they had or wish they had for technical training and changes to training that could help address key challenges or barriers to success. (See Appendix D for the full protocol.)

Upon completion of the focus groups, we conducted systematic coding of the focus group transcripts to identify key themes related to our exploratory questions. Our analysis involved examining topics by AFS to explore the extent to which themes were unique to a specific AFS or group of AFSs or were common across all AFSs.

However, we do not provide percentages or statistical estimates regarding the prevalence of focus group themes. The goal of these focus groups was exploratory in nature, and given the small number of focus groups per AFS and potential for mixed responses within a focus groups, such percentages could be misleading. In addition, not every participant responded to each question asked so it is not possible to provide precise statistical estimates regarding the percentage of individuals who make comments associated with a particular theme. Instead, the goal of these focus groups was to gather rich qualitative information on attitudes, knowledge, and experiences that may provide insight into potential improvements for AFS classification and IST. Additional detail on focus group methodology can be found in Appendix D.

This chapter is organized into two main sections. First, we discuss themes that relate to airmen's knowledge and expectations about their specialties (and IST) before they arrive at IST.

---

[2] Juliet M. Corbin and Anselm L. Strauss, *Basics of Qualitative Research: Techniques and Procedures for Developing Grounded Theory*, 3rd ed., Thousand Oaks, Calif.: Sage Publications, 2008.

These themes were generally consistent across occupational categories. We then describe themes within each occupational category. These themes revolve around the participants' experiences in IST, including what factors relate to student success in their training pipeline, challenges and barriers to success, and how USAF can address those challenges and barriers. Although some of the IST themes cut across occupational categories, there were nuances by occupational category that we wished to capture in our discussion. We end the chapter with a short summary of themes, including those involving IST experiences, that cut across occupational categories.

Knowledge and Expectations About Careers Before Initial Skills Training

Our analysis identified several overarching themes from the focus groups that were consistent across the occupational categories. These themes focus on knowledge and understanding of USAF career options upon joining, understanding of the AFS classification process, and knowledge and expectations of AFS prior to entering IST.

Knowledge and Understanding of Air Force Career Options

Across specialties, airmen in our focus groups described feeling that they had limited knowledge or understanding of different career or specialty options within USAF when they were joining. Recruiters were the most commonly mentioned source of information, but airmen had very mixed responses as to whether the information provided by recruiters was helpful. At the same time, airmen described their experiences as very dependent on the extent to which the recruiter was a member of or familiar with a particular AFS themselves. As one airman stated, "Your recruiter only knows their own job." In cases where the recruiter was not familiar with a particular AFS, airmen described being told to look the information up themselves on the internet and needing to do their own research. Some airmen also described feeling as though they were pushed into or only told about certain specialties based on the recruiter's preferences. As one participant commented,

> I didn't have any information. They just gave us a sheet and were like, pick something from this. So, on my own, I googled the options. I had no idea, so when I came back with my list, I had three options maybe, and everything else was put down for me.

In addition to recruiters, airmen mentioned the importance of the internet as a source of information and, as noted previously, were often told by recruiters to "just google different Air Force jobs" when the recruiter was unfamiliar with different career options. As with their experiences with recruiters, airmen had mixed responses regarding the helpfulness of the official USAF website, with some describing it as too vague.

> I looked at the Air Force website nonstop, but there wasn't too much there. I was basically going off the pictures and descriptions, but the descriptions were vague. I went blind faith in, not knowing what I wanted to do.

Airmen stated that they found online forums such as Reddit and YouTube to provide more detailed and honest information on different jobs, with forums such as Reddit giving them the opportunity to also ask questions to individuals currently serving in those AFSs.

Although mentioned less often, airmen also identified family members and friends as sources of information in cases where those family members and friends were current or former active-duty members and could describe their experiences in different AFSs.

Understanding of Specialty Classification Process

Although airmen discussed having the option to provide a list of their preferred AFSs through their "dream sheets," airmen also described having a limited understanding of how specialties were assigned. Their knowledge was generally limited to understanding that they only qualified for a certain set of specialties and that then the decision was "based on the needs of the Air Force." Some airmen also described feeling as though recruiters often pushed them into certain specialties. One participant commented,

> There's lots of smoke and mirrors in the selection process. . . . It seems like there was a lot of hand waving. Recruiters make you feel like you're obligated to take the job that's offered, and you don't have a choice.

Similarly, another airman, commented:

> Recruiters look out more for themselves than us. It's about numbers for them. They have a quota of jobs they need to fill, and there are jobs the Air Force needs filled.

Knowledge and Expectations of Air Force Specialty Prior to Initial Skills Training

Airmen in our focus groups also had mixed responses regarding knowledge of what to expect in training and of their career once they had been assigned an AFS. Generally, airmen cited similar sources and limitations of sources for learning about AFSs in general (e.g., recruiters and the internet). When asked about what (if any) information they learned in BMT, some airmen mentioned a job book that provided general information, but its helpfulness was described as mixed. Other than that resource, airmen described their experiences in BMT as being very dependent on whether their military training instructors (MTIs) belonged to their AFS or knew of others in their AFS. Most of the airmen in our focus groups who responded to this question indicated that they did not have an MTI who could provide any information to them about their AFS. The one exception to this was airmen in security forces, who mentioned having MTIs who were in their AFS. This was also the only AFS for which airmen mentioned having a separate meeting at BMT to discuss their AFS and what to expect. Overall, though, given a general lack of information, airmen generally described not knowing what to expect during their training. It is also important to note that this was especially true for those airmen who were open general and did not receive their assigned specialty until later in BMT.

In the next section, we dive deeper into each AFS and airmen's experiences in IST, including potential barriers to success.

Findings by Occupational Category

To provide context for the focus group findings for each occupational category, we first provide a brief description of the relevant specialties in terms of general duties and features of technical training pipeline(s). Additional details on this AFS's entry requirements and reclassification rates are provided in Appendix D.

Aerospace Medical Service

Aerospace Medical Service (4N0X1) airmen perform patient care and treatment using knowledge and skills in emergency care, nursing, and primary care and must be able to provide in-flight medical care, as well as medical support in contingency operations and disasters.[3]

The specialty's technical training lasts about 98 days.[4] Students undergo academic and practical (hands-on) training covering topics such as medical terminology, anatomy, and physiology; basic life support; and emergency medical technician (EMT). Students must pass an EMT certification examination to graduate training.[5]

Focus Group Findings

We heard very mixed responses regarding both whether airmen wanted to enter the Aerospace Medical Service specialty and whether the specialty was what they expected, primarily due to a lack of information on the specialty. In terms of experiences in IST, Aerospace Medical Service students highlighted several factors they felt contributed to success in their training pipeline. First, they noted that students' individual characteristics play a role, such as having the drive and motivation to succeed. One participant commented, "The reason why you joined the Air Force, it pushes me." Other individual characteristics or attributes described include having the commitment to put in the necessary time to study and the focus to ignore distractions as well as being able to manage stress well. In addition to individual characteristics, some students in our focus groups noted that peers can be a support during technical training. One student noted,

> If you feel like people are struggling, then you help them. I think that's why we had such a high pass rate in our group.

---

[3] AFPC, 2018, p. 266.

[4] U.S. Air Force, "Aerospace Medical Service," webpage, undated a.

[5] Aerospace Medical Service Apprentice (AMSA) Curriculum Plan, Fort Sam Houston, Tex.: Medical Education and Training Campus, October 29, 2018.

Focus group participants also commented that instructors who put in the extra effort to adjust teaching approaches to align with student learning styles and provide extra assistance to students contribute to successful training completion. One student stated,

> The instructors are awesome, staying after and motivating us. They came into our dorms and practiced skills with us.

When asked about challenges faced in technical training and reasons Aerospace Medical Service students washback or washout, focus group participants cited issues having mainly to do with the training environment outside of the classroom. Participants described military training leaders (MTLs) adding stress by mandating strict regulations in the dorms and imposing punishments for infractions that students found trivial and unrelated to technical training (e.g., stringent standards for keeping dorm rooms clean). This added stress in the dorms can take students' focus and time away from the technical demands of training. One participant commented,

> Dorm life is too important. People come to class and are stuffed with knowledge and then have to go back to the dorms where there are a bunch of regulations. I can see how it's important because we need to transition to that mentality for operations, but I think they could be more understanding. Like when your GPA's [grade point average is] not good, you get all this paperwork to do, then computers are slow, the dryers don't work, there's no AC [air conditioning]. It all adds up on your plate.

Participants also noted that students in the dorms were from a variety of AFSs, many of which they perceived as not as demanding as Aerospace Medical Service and requiring less study time. However, all students, regardless of the technical training requirements and demands of their specialty, had to undergo the same level of activities and regulations outside of the classroom. In addition to these outside environment concerns, focus group participants also stated that some students washout because they have poor time-management skills and do not study as much as needed. Participants could not clearly identify activities that did or could have helped prepare them for success in technical training beyond some college class experience. Some students described college experience as providing confidence and good study habits that contributed to success regardless of class topic; however, classes related to the medical field (e.g., biology, anatomy) were considered more beneficial.

Participants suggested a few changes to the current Aerospace Medical Services technical training to address some of the challenges and reasons for washback or washout they identified. Several students suggested minimizing the amount of out-of-class activities and regulations that are required but unrelated to the content of technical training. Participants felt that this would reduce stress and allow their focus to remain on learning course content. Additionally, some participants raised concerns about the EMT portion of the technical training. Students felt that there should be less focus on the EMT training because it is unlikely to be used in their jobs, as they have been told they are more likely to use nursing skills. One participant commented,

> They should focus more on what we're actually going to be doing, not the EMT part. That part is stressful and knocks a lot of people out. There are people who want to be here who can't get past [EMT training]. And they say we're not even going to be EMTs, just nursing.

Others suggested that the EMT portion of technical training should be lengthened because it is too difficult to learn such a large amount of material in such a short amount of time.

Air Traffic Control

Air Traffic Control (ATC; 1C1X1) "controls en route and terminal air traffic by use of visual, radar, and non-radar means."[6] ATC technical training takes 72 days to complete.[7] It includes a single apprentice course with academic and simulator-based activities, the latter of which occur in the radar and tower blocks of instruction.[8]

Focus Group Findings

Compared with the other AFS focus groups, most ATC airmen in our focus groups mentioned wanting to be in ATC or at least having it somewhere on their list. In terms of experiences in IST, focus groups with ATC students identified key factors that contributed to success in their training pipeline. Students' individual characteristics were noted as being important, and, in particular, having confidence was key. Students observed that the high-stress nature of ATC training requires a thick skin and confidence to thrive. One participant noted,

> When I came into Block 3, I was super timid, and I failed. I came back with confidence and I passed.

Participants also commented that being motivated and putting in the effort to study is critical to success. One student stated,

> The nice thing about ATC is that you don't have to be the smartest guy in the room, but . . . if you're motivated and have the drive and self-awareness, you'll do well. You don't have to be book smart—you can have a high school degree but so long as you have the motivation, you'll be fine.

In addition to individual characteristics, participants also highlighted the importance of the support of peers as contributing to success in technical training. One participant described how peers play a role in this training pipeline:

> For the radar and tower blocks, you as a class need to come together. You might think you're saying something right and someone will catch you saying something wrong. You need your peers to get through this and do better.

In terms of challenges and potential reasons students washback or washout of technical training, ATC students' individual characteristics factor in significantly according to focus group participants. Participants described the high-pressure nature of the ATC job and noted

---

[6] AFPC, 2018, p. 42.

[7] U.S. Air Force, "Air Traffic Control," webpage, undated c.

[8] Information about content of ATC technical training was provided by ATC career field and training staff, as well as focus group participants. Discussions with staff were held in April–May 2019, while focus groups were held in June 2019.

that students who are not resilient or do not deal well with stressful situations will likely struggle in this training and potentially fail. One participant detailed the high-stakes nature of the career field:

> If you do something incorrectly now in this career field, you can be prosecuted and held liable. Here it's such a big deal that it makes you realize that you could be going to jail if you made that mistake in the real world. . . . It makes you think—wow, anything I do wrong can be the end.

Participants also noted that students who do not stay motivated or put in the time to study will not be successful in technical training. Like the Aerospace Medical Service focus group participants, those in ATC talked about the negative impacts of the environment outside the classroom on technical training success. Students complained that they were wasting valuable time that could be spent studying on required activities unrelated to the content of their technical training (e.g., marching and PT). This adds stress and deflects focus from learning the ATC job. Additionally, participants expressed frustration that MTLs, who were all from other career fields did not understand the difficulty of and stress related to ATC technical training. One participant described this challenge:

> Our MTLs have no idea what it's like to be ATC. They have jobs like personnel. They have no idea how hard this career field is. They don't know what we go through or understand the pressure. They expect more from us and add to it when we just want to learn our jobs and get out of here. They can't just release ATCs to be MTLs but if they could get MTLs to see how hard our training is and the work we have to do, they'd be more understanding.

Although ATC participants could not identify any preparation they had prior to training that had contributed to their success, many did note that they wished they had received more information about technical training ahead of time and saw other AFSs receiving this type of information at BMT. One participant commented,

> Before coming to training I would have liked to have had more documents or information on the pace of training or how training works. I imagined the courses would be on simulators but had no idea what to expect.

ATC students suggested changes to training aimed to address challenges or barriers to success in technical training. Like Aerospace Medical Service students, ATC focus group participants recommended minimizing required out of class activities not related to the technical content of training. One participant wished that

> the squadron [did not] keep us so long. [The MTLs] show up late getting to us, we're sitting outside at parade rest. We lose an hour of studying. What are we doing? How does that help? If you don't know the chain of command, you have to do squats. It takes 45 minutes to do this and then we get dinner. We've been out of class for two hours and now that's time you've missed out on studying.

Participants also suggested limiting early wake-up times for these types of activities, which cut into students' sleep and make them tired and less able to focus in class. Additionally, participants suggested that MTLs be trained to understand the nature of ATC technical training demands. Beyond minimizing these types of activities, participants recommended that simulators be available in the dorms so that students can practice outside of the classroom and improve their skills. One participant described this suggested change:

> If there was any way to get some kind of tower simulations in the dorms—that's the only way to get better. . . . We have old-school static boards where you take a notecard with a plane's name down. It works for phraseology, but you don't get the same visual cue. Great, I know what to say, but now everything is moving [in class]. So basically that's one try a day [in class] and you have to pay attention to 12–15 things at once. I know [a simulator] is super expensive but there has to be something.

While mentioned less often than limiting required outside activities and providing simulators in the dorms, changing the order of technical training components was another suggestion. Students recommended switching the order of the radar and tower block, so that tower comes before radar. Some recommended this change because they described tower as a more challenging block and that it should come sooner rather than later to see if students are cut out for ATC earlier in the training pipeline and avoid washing out near the end of training. Others thought having tower first would also help students better understand the radar block. One participant commented,

> Tower is so fast-paced. It doesn't make sense to have the easier block first. If you can't handle Block 5 [tower] then you wasted all your time because you need both [tower and radar]. It doesn't make sense to have the hardest one be last because then you can get washed out and would have wasted three months of training.

Career Enlisted Aviation

For our focus groups, Career Enlisted Aviation (CEA) included three specialties. Airborne Mission Systems Operators (1A3X1) perform a variety of aircrew duties on different platforms, including "operat[ing], maintain[ing], repair[ing], and test[ing] airborne communications, electro-optical sensor, radar, computer, electronic protection (EP) systems, and electronic warfare (EW) systems."[9] Airmen in the Aircraft Loadmaster specialty (1A2X1) oversee cargo and passenger load activities on aircraft, such as checking load placement, reviewing documentation for loads, and supervising loading and unloading.[10] Special Missions Aviation (1A9X1) personnel perform a variety of functions that overlap with the other two CEA specialties but with a focus on special missions.[11]

---

[9] AFPC, 2018, p. 23.

[10] AFPC, 2018, p. 21.

[11] AFPC, 2018, p. 33.

All three CEA specialties take the Aircrew Fundamentals Course for technical training. The course is roughly a month in length.[12] While technical training for the Aircraft Loadmaster and Special Missions Aviation specialties is considered complete after taking this course, students in the Airborne Mission Systems Operator pipeline are required to follow up with the Airborne Mission Systems Operator course, which lengthens their training by a few days.[13] All three specialties also have flying training segments in their training pipelines.

Focus Group Findings

Generally, airmen in the CEA specialties indicated they had put this AFS somewhere on their list, although it may not have always been at the top. In terms of experiences in IST, CEA students who participated in focus groups identified similar factors that contribute to success as ATC and Aerospace Medical Service students. One of the critical factors contributing to success was students having the discipline and drive to put in the necessary study time. One participant stated,

> You have to do it on your end. Spend a few hours every night doing problems. If I hadn't taken the time to study, I wouldn't have made it this far. You just have to put in your end of the work, and you'll be fine.

Participants also described the importance of studying with peers for support, another common theme in other AFSs. One participant noted,

> Most successful people notice that study groups help. You take it back to the dorms and study together for a few hours and build on each other. I think that's why I failed a test before—I didn't know to reach out [to peers]. I think it's a big thing—knowing how to reach out and organize in the first place before issues come up.

Participants noted that engagement with instructors can also support success in technical training. Students reported that most instructors took the time to explain concepts well and also provided helpful insights from the field. One participant commented,

> What helps me is that since we're so personable with our instructors, they monologue a lot. Our teachers have been in our specialty. They know a lot about the blocks and talk about it. It helps me understand the specifics.

Career Enlisted Aviation technical training challenges or potential reasons for washing back or washing out were also similar to those identified by students in other AFSs discussed previously. CEA students described an environment outside of the classroom that was not

---

[12] We retrieved information about the three CEA specialty training requirements from USAF's official website, airforce.com. The website allows users to search for information about AFSs, including technical training length and names of training courses. However, the website does not provide details about course content, so we were limited to providing information about names of courses and pipeline length.

[13] See U.S. Air Force, "Airborne Mission Systems Specialist," webpage, undated b.

conducive to supporting good study habits. Focus group participants expressed frustration with sharing dorm rooms with students from technical training in other career fields that they perceived as less demanding. One participant described this issue:

> The hard thing is there are other AFSs. They aren't serious at all. They aren't studying and can still pass tests. They go party every night and you want to do it too but you have to study.

Participants commented that they were subjected to the same out-of-class requirements as other AFSs such as strict room inspections for cleanliness, but that they were held to a higher standard in the classroom than other students. Beyond these environment-related challenges, focus group participants noted that many students washout simply because they manage their time poorly, have poor study habits, and do not know when to ask for help. For example, one participant commented,

> The people who failed that block, they didn't really apply themselves. They were going out on the weekends and not studying or paying attention in class. It goes back to not staying engaged or holding yourself accountable.

Finally, participants described challenges with the amount of material students are required to learn in a limited amount of time. Some students fall behind and are unable to keep up with the pace. One participant described this challenge:

> They say over and over that it's like a firehose of information. So, you just have to drink it up somehow.

A few focus group participants did note that some education or experience helped them prepare for success in training. For example, high school math courses and basic aviation courses or aerodynamics, as well as experience with computers were all mentioned as having helped students prepare and succeed. One participant stated,

> I think it's mostly knowing how to add, subtract, some algebra, remember order of operations, and don't forget the decimal point. If you know what all that is, you're solid.

Another participant commented,

> I know the computer block I had was pretty easy because I had a background in it. It was just a hobby of mine, but I knew how to build a computer when I was younger.

Some participants noted that they would have liked to have had more information about CEA technical training requirements so they could have prepared and studied some relevant content ahead of time. One participant describes this as follows:

> Most of it, like factoring, I learned a while back and haven't thought about it for 6 years because it's not relevant to my life. It would've been nice for the Air Force to say, "For this job you should brush up on this." I would've done that in DEP—just open a few books and study. I think a lot of us would have.

Focus group participants also suggested changes to improve CEA technical training. Like students in other AFSs, many recommended changes improving the environment outside of the classroom. While participants suggested limiting out-of-class activities that cut into students' time for studying course material, the most prominent recommendation was to ensure dorm roommates are from the same AFS training pipeline. One participant stated,

> Something they could fix is make sure you're roomed with someone in the same career field. We all study like crazy [in CEA] and I have two roommates in different career fields that are up late playing video games and loud music when I'm trying to sleep. They don't have to study as hard but when they were studying it was a lot easier for me. If we [CEAs] were all together, we'd be studying at the same times.

Additionally, participants noted that male students are unable to study with female students outside of class because they are in separate dorms that they are not allowed to enter. Participants suggested that dorms should have common areas for studying where male and female students can study together. One stated,

> Males can't go into female dorms and vice versa. You can study outside but who's going to do that? The library is on the other side of the base. There's not another place to study with other sexes. I feel like it leaves her [indicating female focus group participant] out.

Other suggested changes focused on the timing of CEA technical training. Some participants recommended that extra time be built into technical training so that some of the more difficult blocks were longer to allow more time to learn this material. Participants also suggested that the technical training be altered to provide more flexibility in terms of timing and schedule. For example, if instructors found that students were struggling with a certain block, they could extend it by a day or two, but if students picked up the content of another block quickly, they could move forward ahead of schedule. One participant described this suggested change:

> I think it could be improved. For different blocks there are set days and a graduation date and full time they want us to be here. I think they're so worried about getting blocks done in that certain amount of time, you can teach it and test how normally you would, but you can put it at a pace that works. Sometimes everyone gets it in one day, but then another day no one gets it and yet we still have to test.

Focus group participants also expressed a desire for more hands-on training during IST, which was described by one CEA student as follows:

> Earlier hands-on training. One of our instructors had old computer parts that he would pass around. During one review game I was able to see the physical computer piece that was the answer. It helps me to see it in addition to reading it.

Finally, like students from other occupational categories in our focus groups, CEA focus group participants noted that better information about the CEA career fields and technical training would help students be better prepared. Being aware of IST requirements would potentially provide opportunities to prepare prior to attending IST as well as reducing stress for students while in training.

Cyber

Similar to CEA, Cyber focus groups involved three specialties. Client Systems (3D1X1) airmen perform "client-level information technology support functions" such as "install[ing] and configur[ing] software operating systems and applications."[14] Cyber Systems Operations (3D0X2) airmen "install and support . . . systems to ensure they operate properly and remain secure from outside intrusion."[15] Finally, each airman in Cyber Transport Systems (3D1X2) "provides voice, data and video services" such as "install[ing], upgrad[ing], replac[ing], configur[ing] and maintain[ing] systems/circuits/[internet protocol]-based intrusion detection/long haul communications systems that access military, federal and commercial networks."[16]

All three of the cyber specialties have technical training consisting of information-technology (IT) fundamentals (same for all cyber specialties), an AFS-specific course, and an IT security course with a commercial certification test required for graduation.[17] Client Systems and Cyber Systems Operations pipelines are of similar length (just short of 70 days), whereas the training pipeline for Cyber Transport Systems lasts for 136 days.[18]

Focus Group Findings

Overall, we heard mixed responses regarding whether airmen wanted to enter the different cyber AFSs. In terms of experiences in IST, participants from cyber specialties shared some of the same factors for success in IST as students from other AFSs previously discussed. For example, cyber students noted individuals' ability to be self-motivated, driven, and disciplined as being critical to success in technical training for cyber AFSs. One participant commented,

> If you're a self-motivated person that's the best thing. The ability to sit down and focus yourself.

---

[14] AFPC, 2018, p. 203.

[15] U.S. Air Force, "Cyber Systems Operations," webpage, undated e.

[16] AFPC, 2018, p. 205.

[17] Information based on Air Force training pipeline slides from 2015, as well as information provided by cyber focus group participants in April 2019.

[18] Client Systems information can be found at U.S. Air Force, "Client Systems," webpage, undated d. Cyber Systems Operations information can be found at U.S. Air Force, "Cyber Systems Operations," webpage, undated e. Cyber Transport Systems information can be found at U.S. Air Force, "Cyber Transport Systems," webpage, undated f.

Participants also identified relationships with peers, such as joining study groups, as contributing to success in training. Participants commented on the ways students help one another out during training:

> [You get] motivation from students in the higher blocks. They will tell you it's passable and doable, giving you confidence, and telling you which chapters to focus on without giving up too much information about the specifics. We had a friend who went out of his way to create a website to tell us what to concentrate on. It helps.

Beyond peers, participants noted that some instructors make themselves available for support in training. Instructors who adapt their approach based on the learning styles of students can be particularly helpful. Many participants also described the self-paced nature of some of the cyber career field technical training as contributing to success. One participant stated,

> I like self-paced. You can go as fast as you want and understand the information at a pace that suits you.

Another participant similarly commented,

> They set it up so that you can take the tests or knowledge checks when you're ready. I think that's better—it works in everyone's favor.

However, a few participants did note that the self-paced nature of some of the coursework can potentially add stress for some students who feel they are falling behind or prefer to have instructors review concepts with them for better comprehension.

When asked about technical training challenges or reasons for washing back or washing out, students from cyber career fields most often identified the Security Plus certification requirement, which comes at the end of IST training. They saw it as very difficult to pass, the most challenging portion of technical training, and often the reason students fail. One participant commented, "Sec[urity] Plus is 90 percent of reclassification." Another participant stated,

> The blocks kind of set you up for failure. Everything is super easy, but then you take Sec+ [Security Plus certification] and it's a monster. It's a false sense of security.

Cyber students also expressed frustration with not having enough time to prepare for the Security Plus certification requirement and noted that civilians in the IT field had a great deal of experience prior to obtaining the certification. One participant described this challenge as follows:

> Sec+ [Security Plus certification] is structured poorly. You study a completely different subject and then you have two weeks to prepare for Sec[urity] Plus when you're supposed to have three years of IT experience [in the civilian world]. I feel like that's not a good mechanism to get through this training.

Beyond the Security Plus requirement, participants in cyber technical training identified challenges similar to those identified by students in other AFSs. For example, cyber students described the environment outside of class and in the dorms as stressful and involving activities that students perceive as a waste of time and taking their focus away from studying. One participant commented,

> I would see people in class trying to study and other people would be worried about taking the trash out or leaving a light on in their rooms. They're sitting there, freaking out, and worrying that they forgot something in their room and they'll get in trouble for it. It's a huge distraction. They shouldn't be thinking about that. They should be able to concentrate on studying.

Focus group participants also identified characteristics of students that can contribute to difficulties in training, such as having poor time management skills and not focusing on studying. For example, one participant noted,

> Distractions. I play video games. Doing stuff in your free time can limit your ability to study. The people failing are the ones who aren't separating themselves from the distractions. Like I said, I play video games from time to time, but I know when to turn it off and study.

Additional challenges identified were related to instructors and resources. While some instructors were noted as supporting students' success in training, other instructors were described as not providing enough help to students, especially regarding preparing for Security Plus certification, and some were perceived as lacking comprehensive knowledge in some of the training subject areas. Some participants noted that a shortage of instructors contributed to the limited time they had available to provide extra help and also to best align their skillsets to the course topic. One participant commented,

> There's obviously a manning issue. Some of [the instructors] are not qualified to teach every block and they get thrown in and they're not prepared to teach that block.

Another participant stated,

> Most instructors seem poorly trained or inconsistently trained. If you were in a college setting you wouldn't want to pay for this quality of instruction. Good instructors are going to help you pass the test, but even with the good ones, once you ask them something a little outside the box, they have no idea. You're learning what's in the textbook but that's it.

Some focus group participants relayed that specific types of prior education, such as computer science or IT courses, did help them in portions of technical training for cyber AFSs. One participant commented,

> I had a little computer science, so I understood binary and had some experience on how this worked at a basic level. I think that was helpful. Block one was easy [for me]. Others struggled but I could move on.

Many participants noted that they believed receiving more information about technical training requirements ahead of time would have helped them be successful and overcome some challenges in training. Specifically, students described wanting to have been informed about the

Security Plus certification requirement so they could have begun preparing before technical training began. One stated,

> They could have said, "Hey, there's a course called Sec[urity] Plus and we advise you to study." I could have read the book, looked at YouTube, taken quizzes and been better set up. It would have been nice to know just to prepare ourselves for the future. For me, being prepared and being ahead is just something you strive for.

Not surprisingly, when suggesting changes to technical training, participants recommended providing more time to prepare for the Security Plus exam to improve student success rates in training and alleviate some of the stress related to learning such a large amount of complex material in a short time at the end of training. One participant commented,

> I think a good compromise is at least expanding the Sec[urity] Plus course. Ten days or two work weeks isn't enough time. Civilians who qualify for Sec[urity] Plus have two years. Every person who washes out is wasting at least $600 not to mention the cost of teaching them the regular training pipeline [prior to Security Plus].

Other participants suggested integrating Security Plus preparation throughout IST rather than concentrating it at the end or moving the requirement to the first duty station as on the job training. Other changes to training recommended included themes similar to those reported by students from other AFSs such as reducing out-of-class mandated activities that take time and focus away from studying as well as making the dorm environment more conducive to studying by keeping similar AFSs together as roommates and ensuring MTLs understand training requirements. One participant stated,

> We only have one MTL who passed Sec[urity] Plus so there's only one person who can talk to us about that. The rest [of our MTLs] are maintenance and not even from cyber so there aren't really people with experience from whom we can get advice. More MTLs should actually be cybers.

Participants also suggested having instructors more consistently provide assistance to students when needed outside of regular classroom instruction.

Security Forces

Security Forces protect and defend personnel, equipment, and resources on USAF bases as well as in deployed environments.[19] Security Forces IST is about 65 days.[20]

Focus Group Findings

We heard very mixed responses regarding whether airmen wanted to enter security forces. In terms of experiences in IST, while focus group participants from security forces technical

---

[19] AFPC, 2018, p. 243.

[20] U.S. Air Force, "Security Forces," webpage, undated i.

training had a few themes in common with students from other AFSs when describing their experiences, security forces students' experiences and perspectives did differ somewhat from those in other AFSs. When asked about what factors contribute to success in training, studying was not named as a factor, unlike with students in other AFSs discussed previously. Security forces students noted that individuals having a positive attitude and being disciplined and motivated helped them succeed. For example, one participant commented,

> People who want to be here contribute to success. When people are here as a last resort, they don't want to be here and have a glass half empty view. They bring us down.

Additionally, focus group participants noted that support from peers and students who are good team players contributed to success in security forces technical training. For example, one participant stated,

> Having peers. We're all from different places but when you feel like you're together and have friends who will have your back and someone who cares about you, it's easy. Well, it's not easy but it makes it better.

Security forces students also identified challenges with technical training and reasons students might washback or washout. Participants commented that some students struggled with motivation and that that could result in disciplinary issues. For example, one participant commented,

> [The reason for washout] could be disciplinary. Some people lose their minds after BMT. You get your freedoms back like phone, family, free time, and they start breaking phase, they keep breaking phase, and lose form. After a while they're done.

Another participant noted how disciplinary issues can negatively affect students' motivation:

> You get put on tango for disciplinary. If you're on it long enough, you lose motivation and aren't part of the team. Then you keep misbehaving and get put on tango again.[21]

Similarly, some participants identified injuries as a challenge for a number of students, as well as a possible reason for washing back. For example, one participant cited a situation in which

> people get hurt and put on x-ray. The reason they're on x-ray is to get better to rejoin their team. But they lose motivation if they washback because they have to stay here longer and meet new people they never have met before.

---

[21] Tango refers to a status that airmen get placed into when they have disciplinary infractions in training. Based on the context of discussions with airmen, those placed on tango status are removed from the training for a period of time.

Participants also expressed frustration with the environment at technical training, which they perceived as wasting a good deal of time without providing useful instruction. One participant commented,

> I like the training . . . but there's a lot of wasted time. We stand around a lot. Accountability checks every night, meet up on the drill pad, count off, count CACs. Sometimes it's quick—30 minutes—and other times it takes two hours. It eats a lot of time.

Additionally, some participants found the environment challenging in that it was unnecessarily hard on them and the manner in which students were treated added too much stress. Participants also expressed that this type of environment can hurt morale:

> Since the first day, they tell our team we suck. It gets into everyone's head so they can't get past it. Like when you beat a dog too much and raise your hand toward it, it just runs away.

Despite these challenges, some participants pointed out that they did not feel the training was difficult, a sentiment rarely expressed in focus groups with students from other AFSs. One participant noted,

> [IST] is not that hard. . . . We're running a lot but it's not that bad. I can't think of anything else [that's difficult].

When asked if anything did help or could have helped students better prepare for technical training for security forces, focus group participants identified only physical preparation. Participants observed that students in good physical shape had an advantage in training, and some noted they wished they had worked out more prior to training to better prepare for the physical requirements.

The changes to security forces technical training that focus group participants related primarily to the training environment outside of the classroom. Despite participants earlier identifying disciplinary issues as a reason some students washback or washout, participants suggested the training environment be less restrictive in terms of students' freedoms and personal time. One participant commented,

> The base thing is too restrictive. People want to rebel. Just being able to wear your own clothes to walk two minutes to eat dinner would be nice. Make things a little less restrictive.

Another stated,

> They say to enjoy our weekends, but our curfew is at 10:15 p.m. We are grown adults, this sucks. Literally they tell us to enjoy our weekends, but we have to worry about getting back on base on time.

Participants also recommended that activities that are perceived by students to be a waste of time, such as accountability, be limited. Similarly, some participants suggested that classroom lectures could be shortened and that some instructors were wasting time in class telling personal anecdotes rather than focusing explicitly on course content.

Summary

While technical training has unique characteristics for each occupational category, there are common themes students across occupational categories identified. First, airmen described having limited information about specialties both upon joining the USAF and after they had been assigned a specialty. They also cited a lack of information about the overall classification process. In particular, the information they received from recruiters and BMT was dependent on the extent to which their recruiter or MTI had personal experience with the specialty.

According to focus group participants across most of the occupational categories, success in IST is driven primarily by (1) individuals' ability to self-motivate and have the drive to commit to studying and (2) engagement with peers through study groups and teamwork, as well as support from instructors. The main challenges in technical training and reasons why students washback or washout include students having poor study habits, lacking discipline, or not handling stress well.

Additionally, students across occupational categories described challenges that were part of the training environment outside of the classroom and that added stress. Participants noted that required activities unrelated to the content of technical training (e.g., marching) take time away from studying or simply from downtime to recharge. Dorm life was also perceived as not conducive to studying and supporting success in training (e.g., having roommates from less-demanding specialties). Participants suggested changes to technical training to address these external environment stressors such as minimizing requirements out of the classroom and making dorm life more conducive to studying for students.

Finally, students desired more information about technical training and its requirements prior to attending IST in order to better prepare. As discussed previously, overall input from security forces students was the primary outlier compared with focus group participants from other occupational categories, as physical requirements were identified as the focus of training rather than course content that necessitates significant time studying outside of the classroom.

7. Conclusions and Recommendations

Every year, thousands of people enlist in USAF and are classified into hundreds of enlisted occupational specialties. Although most airmen successfully complete IST, about 10 percent are eliminated. These eliminated airmen are either separated from USAF or reclassified into other AFSCs. Given recent increases in reclassification, we set out to identify factors that may influence IST success and to determine if USAF classification and reclassification processes can be improved. The earlier chapters of this report document our analyses and findings. In this chapter, we provide an overview of the key findings and conclude with a series of recommendations focused on data, data quality, and selection and classification processes. In most cases, the recommendations are mutually exclusive of any decision to implement ML. That is, many recommendations can be adopted now to improve the USAF classification and reclassification system.

Key Findings

In this section, we outline four primary findings from the quantitative and qualitative analyses.

Increasing the Number of Relevant Predictor Variables Can Increase the Accuracy of ML Predictions

Based on our analyses comparing different ML models, we found that increasing the set of predictor variables may provide substantial gains in prediction accuracy but that the type of ML model used did not have much of an impact on prediction accuracy. Specifically, the ML models often differed by less than 1 percent when comparing errors in predicting outcomes. However, expanding the set of predictor variables in the ML models generally decreased prediction errors by approximately 5 percent.

Initial Skills Training Classification Is Designed to Optimize Training Success but Not Other Important Outcomes

IST graduation rates have been consistently high over the past decade or so for most specialties. With average graduation rates often above 95 percent, further efforts to optimize training success may yield minimal gains. However, our analyses demonstrate that ML models may be more effective for predicting other important outcomes such as early separation and reenlistment.

Reclassification Is a Manual Process and Can Be Optimized to Achieve Different Outcomes

Our findings reveal that USAF uses a manual process for reclassification, beginning with the schoolhouse command deciding that a student should be eliminated from a training pipeline and reclassified into another through 2AF's role in determining minimum qualifications of the airman and training seat availability. To determine if there could be cost savings or improvements in training and career outcomes by an alternative process for reclassifications, we ran a series of optimization models. Our optimization modeling suggests that USAF might not be using the minimal cost solution for IST reclassifications or the solution that produces the maximum number of positive training and career outcomes. Although reclassifying airmen with optimization models to achieve optimal training and career outcomes is possible, achieving these results will increase the costs of reclassification. Alternative solutions that achieve slightly better training and career outcomes while also reducing the costs currently associated with reclassification are also possible.

Focus Groups Identify Gaps in Air Force Information About Airmen Characteristics, Training Environment, and Job Activities

Based on our focus groups with airmen in IST for select specialties, we identified themes in what airmen know and expect about specialties prior to IST, what factors may affect IST success (and failure), and suggestions for ways USAF can help airmen succeed in IST. Themes involving what airmen knew and expected about their specialties and training prior to IST cut across all five occupational categories that we included in the focus groups. Themes related to IST experiences varied by occupational category, although some themes cut across several occupational categories. Table 7.1 provides a high-level summary of the cross-cutting themes involving IST success, challenges, and areas to improve student success.

The cross-cutting (but not universal) themes in Table 7.1 suggest that specialties with heavy course loads and high levels of technical requirements require students who are motivated, disciplined, and can handle stress; have knowledgeable and supportive instructors; have opportunities to study with peers outside of class time; and have fewer distractions that take away from study time and rest outside the classroom (e.g., dorm roommates who are partying instead of studying). Cross-cutting themes on suggested improvements focus on IST specifics (i.e., pipeline changes and giving airmen more details on IST requirements before they go to IST) as well as the environment outside the classroom (i.e., reducing requirements outside the classroom and assigning dorm roommates according to their specialties). The suggested improvements are based on student input but have not been examined to determine if they would actually improve their success in training. As we discuss later in this chapter, further review of the technical training environment would be needed to determine which areas of improvement merit consideration.

Table 7.1. Cross-Cutting Focus Group Themes About Initial Skills Training Success, Challenges, and Suggested Improvements

Theme	Occupational Category				
	Aerospace Medical Service	ATC	Career Enlisted Aviation	Cyber	Security Forces
IST Success					
Airmen characteristics and experiences					
Motivated, disciplined, resilient	X	X	X	X	X
Prior education and/or experiences (e.g., math courses)	X		X	X	
Supportive/engaged instructors	X	X	X	X	
Study groups		X	X	X	
IST Challenges					
Airmen not focused on studying, not able to handle stress of IST	X	X	X	X	
Training base environment					
Too much time needed for out-of-class activities (e.g., accountability checks)	X	X	X	X	X
Distractions from roommates with lighter course loads	X	X	X	X	
Insufficient resources for group study outside class time		X		X	
Suggested Changes to Improve Student Success in IST					
Add time to and/or change order of IST instructional blocks	X	X	X	X	
Reduce USAF requirements that occur outside class time	X	X	X	X	X
Assign dorm roommates with same AFSs			X	X	
Provide more information about IST requirements in advance (e.g., while airmen are in BMT)		X	X	X	

Recommendations

In the following sections, we outline four sets of recommendations to improve USAF enlisted classification and reclassification:

- expand the set of predictors and outcomes used in USAF enlisted classification
- improve data quality, comprehensiveness, and access
- update classification processes
- address common ML challenges prior to implementation.

Expand the Set of Predictors and Outcomes Used in Air Force Enlisted Classification

Our first set of recommendations emphasize the importance of using high quality predictor and outcome variables. We offer several specific recommendations but recognize that there are costs and resources required to implement each one. Therefore, we prioritize recommendations loosely in order of increasing level of resources required to implement. New predictors should be carefully evaluated prior to implementation to ensure their utility is justified.

Predictors

Archive Technical Training Management System–Job Match and Other Relevant Data Used to Qualify Airmen for Air Force Specialties

Machine learning works by learning patterns that exist in historical data. Although USAF personnel databases maintain hundreds of variables that could be evaluated in a statistical model, critical data in TTMS-JM are not retained after airmen graduate from IST. These data include information used to determine if airmen not only are qualified but are a potentially good match for career specialties. Therefore, we recommend ensuring that these data and any other relevant information used to qualify airmen for occupational specialties be retained in a database format accessible to future analysis.

Require All Recruits to Complete the Air Force Work Interest Navigator and Recruiters to Use Results to Educate Recruits

Airmen in our focus groups described feeling that they had limited knowledge or understanding of different career or specialty options within USAF when they were joining. However, personnel research suggests that vocational interests can help to guide career choices and are important predictors of training performance, job satisfaction, and retention. USAF is already investing in a vocational interests inventory, AF-WIN. Initial analyses conducted by the Strategic Research and Assessment Branch (DSYX) in AFPC provide preliminary support for using AF-WIN to help match airmen to jobs: Airmen were more satisfied with their jobs when assigned to a specialty that matched to a top-ten specialty recommended by AF-WIN. These findings suggest that AF-WIN results may predict airmen work outcomes beyond IST graduation.

AF-WIN was launched in May 2018, but because it is only an optional assessment, only a small percentage of recruits have completed AF-WIN. We recommend requiring all USAF recruits to complete AF-WIN prior to job assignment (i.e., before an enlistment contract is signed) and that recruiters educate recruits on the AF-WIN results, including details about requirements for the specialties. Given that our focus groups revealed that IST students felt they did not have sufficient knowledge about their specialties when they joined, AF-WIN can be used as a communication tool by recruiters.

Systematically Collect Information About Job Requirements

Building on current efforts to identify competencies required across all specialties in USAF (e.g., USAF institutional competencies defined in USAF Manual 36-2647) can help to identify new ways to cluster jobs.[1] As shown in Chapter 4, clustering AFSCs beyond existing MAGE categories can improve the accuracy of prediction models. Therefore, we recommend that USAF develop and evaluate AFSC clusters based on job requirements to further improve ML predictions and matching airmen to specialties.

Develop a Structured Biodata Instrument That Is Completed by All Enlisted Recruits

The process that USAF career field managers use to identify which high school courses are desired for their specialties is unclear and does not appear to be very systematic. Furthermore, some courses provide limited value to prediction models because almost all airmen took the course (e.g., English). We recommend conducting a systematic analysis that gathers inputs from career field SMEs about the relevance of a full range of courses. This analysis could go beyond high school courses and include other relevant background and experiences that may be useful to predicting future performance. Findings from a systematic analysis of desired high school courses and other background experiences could be used by personnel researchers, such as those in AFPC/DSYX, to develop more sophisticated biodata instruments.[2] Although biodata and other self-report inventories can be susceptible to false reporting (i.e., faking), research suggests that biodata faking can be reduced by using items that are verifiable.[3]

Consider Using Peers and BMT Instructors to Rate Personality

Although USAF currently uses TAPAS to assign airmen to a few select career fields, the ML models suggest only limited improvements can be made by integrating TAPAS into prediction models. Given this finding and research that suggests that personality plays a critical role in predicting a variety of important organizational outcomes, we suggest that USAF consider collecting personality ratings from other sources, including peers and instructors at BMT. Peers and instructors should have ample opportunities throughout BMT to observe other airmen's patterns of behavior. Peer ratings of personality are valuable because peers often provide information about how others typically behave when not observed by supervisors/ instructors. Observations of behavior outside of formal settings can be important indicators of personality that could predict organizational citizenship behaviors and counterproductive work

---

[1] U.S. Air Force Manual 36-2647, *Institutional Competency Management and Development*, March 25, 2014.

[2] Michael K. Mount, Lisa A. Witt, and Murray R. Barrick, "Incremental Validity of Empirically Keyed Biodata Scales over GMA and the Five Factor Personality Constructs," *Personnel Psychology*, Vol. 53, No. 2, 2000.

[3] Crystal M. Harold, Lynn A. McFarland, and Jeff A. Weekley, "The Validity of Verifiable and Non-Verifiable Biodata Items: An Examination Across Applicants and Incumbents," *International Journal of Selection and Assessment*, Vol. 14, No. 4, 2006.

behaviors. As a proof of concept, USAF could pilot test this idea in technical training, which tends to have more flexible schedules than BMT.

Systematically Examine the Impact of Training Environment on Airmen's Training Success

Although our optimization analysis suggests that USAF optimizes against training *graduation* as an outcome, there are still areas for improvement within IST. Airmen in our focus groups—particularly those in cognitively demanding specialties—find challenges in the training environments, particularly when they are away from class. As shown in Table 7.1, challenges range from distractions from roommates to additional duties such as accountability checks. Airmen suggested improvements to address these challenges, such as assigning roommates based on specialty so that airmen would have roommates with the same specialty. However, focus groups do not provide sufficient evidence that such changes would be effective or efficient. For example, assigning roommates by specialty may create logistical burdens that outweigh the benefits for airmen. We therefore recommend that USAF systematically examine training environment factors to determine what could be addressed to improve airmen training outcomes.[4]

Outcomes

Define and Systematically Measure Outcomes Beyond Those Associated with Initial Skills Training Success

The vast majority of efforts to improve selection and classification has focused on reducing training attrition, which has led to very high graduation rates in technical training pipelines. Consequently, there is little room to increase prediction accuracy of IST graduation. Put another way, USAF enlisted selection and classification have already been optimized to maximize the probability that airmen will graduate IST. However, initial training success captures only one of many objectives valued by organizations. As we demonstrate in an optimization analysis in Chapter 4, USAF could optimize against other outcomes, such as reenlistment, promotion, and first-term completion. Moreover, USAF could leverage or build on existing surveys to systematically measure workplace attitudes and behaviors identified in personnel research as important for employee success, including organizational citizenship behaviors (e.g., helping others, volunteering), counterproductive work behaviors (e.g., misconduct), and organizational

---

[4] The evaluation approach will depend on types of factors examined and level of evidence that USAF desires. For example, a randomized controlled trial can provide the strongest evidence of the impact of an intervention (e.g., change in roommate assignment process) on outcomes since it rules out selection biases. However, these kinds of studies can be costly to execute. As an alternative, USAF may choose to pull records of student roommate assignments and then run statistical analyses to see if there is a relationship between roommate specialty match and airmen performance outcomes, such as student training grades.

commitment.[5] Classification models could then be developed to consider these outcomes when recommending assignments to airmen.

Monitor the Moving Averages for Graduation by Specialty

Although IST elimination rates have remained relatively stable over the past decade or so, there has been fluctuation in individual specialties. Lessons can be learned by establishing a baseline for each specialty and then monitoring changes against that baseline. If moving average rates (e.g., average graduation rate of 18 months) significantly deviate from the baseline, systematic efforts should be taken to identify the potential root cause(s). These efforts could include conducting interviews with relevant SMEs (e.g., the career field managers, training pipeline managers, and training managers) to determine if changes have been made to the specialty's technical training requirements; holding small group discussions with technical training students in that specialty; and evaluating whether the quality of airmen assigned to the specialty coincides with changes in the graduation rate. Taken together, these data collection efforts may indicate a need to track other reasons for training elimination. Currently, some elimination reasons (e.g., medical) tracked by USAF are quite broad, and understanding whether these eliminations could be prevented through additional screening and/or training would be helpful. Clear definitions and instructions for elimination categories should be provided to reduce potential errors and bias.[6]

Improve Data Quality, Comprehensiveness, and Access

The quality of data is integral to ensure that ML models can provide accurate and useful predictions of future outcomes. However, achieving sufficient data quality is a challenge for organizations because they "often overestimate data quality and underplay the implications of poor quality data," which can lead to "consequences of bad data [that] may range from significant to catastrophic."[7] USAF is not immune to these challenges. In fact, the quantitative researchers on our project team estimate that approximately 80 percent of their time was spent acquiring, merging, and addressing data quality issues. Given the importance of data quality and our estimates, we provide a set of recommendations designed to improve and monitor the quality of data used to develop and implement ML models.

---

[5] Reeshad S. Dalal, "A Meta-Analysis of the Relationship Between Organizational Citizenship Behavior and Counterproductive Work Behavior," *Journal of Applied Psychology*, Vol. 90, No. 6, 2005; Suzy Fox, Paul E. Spector, and Don Miles, "Counterproductive Work Behavior (CWB) in Response to Job Stressors and Organizational Justice: Some Mediator and Moderator Tests for Autonomy and Emotions," *Journal of Vocational Behavior*, Vol. 59, No. 3, 2001.

[6] Michael A. Campion, "Meaning and Measurement of Turnover: Comparison of Alternative Measures and Recommendations for Research," *Journal of Applied Psychology*, Vol. 76, No. 2, 1991.

[7] Venkat Gudivada, Amy Apon, and Junhua Ding, "Data Quality Considerations for Big Data and Machine Learning: Going Beyond Data Cleaning and Transformations," *International Journal on Advances in Software*, Vol. 10, No. 1, 2017.

Use a Data Quality Framework for Selection and Classification Variables

A data quality framework can help USAF to anticipate and address problems in the data used by ML and optimization models. For example, a data quality framework proposed for health care settings includes the following dimensions for evaluating quality of a system's data:

- accuracy: error-free, up-to-date, unambiguous, and meaningful to the users
- completeness: represent all relevant aspects of the system(s) and are relevant to data users' tasks
- accessibility: "authorized and unobstructed" access to data for approved data users
- consistency: format, definitions, and values of data standardized across the system(s)
- nonredundancy: no more than one information system to map data for a given entity
- readability: understandable to users, easy to manipulate for analysis, and including documented information provided about the data (e.g., metadata)
- usefulness: perceived to provide value in achieving intended purpose(s)
- trust: secured "enough against losses and unauthorised [sic] access."[8]

In Chapter 3, we highlighted some of the challenges we encountered with data quality (Table 3.4). Here, we align some of those challenges (and others) along the dimensions of the data quality framework (Table 7.2) in order to help USAF use the framework to determine areas for improvement in data quality.

Table 7.2. Examples of Data Quality Challenges in Air Force Personnel Data

Data Quality Dimension	Example of USAF Personnel Data Challenges
Accuracy	Skill-level dates not always updated, leading to illogical date sequences (e.g., skill-level award date preceding IST graduation date)
Completeness	TTMS-JM data used by Job Spin discarded after students graduate technical training, making the data unavailable for evaluating classification system outcomes
Accessibility	ATC-ST is maintained on one machine and data is kept in only one siloed database at AFPC
Consistency	Definitions for data are not tied to the data but typically reside with a range of SMEs familiar with the different personnel data systems
Nonredundancy	ASVAB data housed in multiple USAF and DoD data systems
Readability	AF Form 125As retained as PDF, not accessible as data to be analyzed
Usefulness	Some variables have very limited variability (e.g., completing high school English class), which are not very useful in analytical models since they do not differentiate among airmen
Trust	Unknown[a]

[a] Trust reflects a system-wide security issue for USAF and would likely be addressed by leadership and content experts trained in information security and technology.

---

[8] See in Lu Bai, Rob Meredith, and Frada Burstein, "A Data Quality Framework, Method and Tools for Managing Data Quality in a Health Care Setting: An Action Case Study," *Journal of Decision Systems*, Vol. 27, No. 1, April 16, 2018, Appendix 1, pp. 153–154.

Establish Data Steward(s) or Custodian(s) to Oversee Data Quality

To address current and potential future concerns with data quality, USAF should consider allocating resources to develop formal positions (e.g., data stewards or custodians) to be responsible for developing data dictionaries, establishing procedures and criteria for ensuring data meet defined quality standards, and developing protocols for preprocessing data prior to integration into analytic models. Other responsibilities could include defining the authoritative source for data elements, managing access, and coordinating the integration of data derived from different sources.

Evaluate the Accuracy and Completeness of Data

Although there are many dimensions to data quality, foremost among them are accuracy and completeness. During our project we found that data from multiple USAF personnel systems varied widely in terms of both dimensions. Databases often contained overlapping variables and for overlapping individuals (i.e., did not meet the data nonredundancy criterion in Table 7.2), but the data often lacked full correspondence, and we could not determine which data should take precedence based on available information. In other cases, data values did not follow logical rules (e.g., enlistment dates following promotion dates, numerical values exceeding score ranges on ASVAB subtests). More subtly, business logic for using variables and tracing changes in variable levels and names over time were poorly documented. None of these data challenges is unique to USAF, and none is insurmountable. Yet they point to the need for deliberate planning to ensure acceptable data standards and management.

Ensure Data Are in a Structured Format

Data must be structured. For example, sections of EPRs and administrative forms for training eliminations (Form 125As) may contain nuanced information about individual performance, but in the form of unstructured text. To be usable for ML, these data first need to be extracted from PDF formats and then be evaluated by natural language processing techniques.

Update Classification and Reclassification Processes to Improve Job-Match Outcomes

The current USAF approach to assigning airmen to specialties emphasizes meeting minimum MAGE requirements, which have served USAF well in predicting IST graduation. However, USAF could consider matching airmen to specialties to optimize other outcomes so that airmen not only succeed in training but are more likely to perform well on the job and be satisfied in their USAF careers. The following recommendations briefly describe a job-match focus for both initial classification and reclassification decisions. Prior to adopting any modifications, USAF should compare the results of new algorithms with Job Spin assignments to ensure intended outcomes are achieved.

Replace Job Spin Inputs with Probabilities for Different Outcomes

Job Spin uses only a limited amount of available information to assign airmen to specialties. As we demonstrated in Chapter 4 and noted earlier in this chapter, there is little room for improving prediction of IST graduation. However, other outcomes, including early separation and reenlistment, offer opportunities for improvement. USAF should consider replacing or augmenting current Job Spin inputs with predicted probabilities of these other outcomes. The amount of weight given to the probabilities can be adjusted over time to meet changing USAF priorities (e.g., increasing reenlistment rates).

Consider Integrating Reclassification Decisions into Job Spin

The process for reclassifying airmen is largely manual and time-consuming. Job Spin could be updated to include airmen who need to be reclassified. The model could give a lower priority to placing reclassified airmen than BMT trainees so that airmen from the latter group are placed into training slots first. The model could also ensure that a sufficient number of training seats are held for current students who may need to be recycled (i.e., who washback).

Consider Expanding the Time Horizon for Assigning Reclassified Airmen

As we note in our observations at the end of Chapter 2 and in our discussion in Chapter 5, reclassification processes are designed to minimize relocation costs and the amount of time that reclassified airmen wait to start training in their new specialty. These are short-term goals and may come at the expense of matching reclassified airmen to specialties in which they may be more satisfied, more committed, and perform better. Our analyses in Chapter 5 show that most training pipelines start within a relatively short period of time (i.e., about 40 days) and if used to match reclassified airmen, could provide long-term gains.

Address Common Machine-Learning Challenges Prior to Implementation

Although the results of the ML analyses from our project demonstrate that gains in prediction accuracy can be made by including relevant predictors, numerous challenges must be overcome before USAF can apply ML models to personnel selection and classification systems at speed and scale. These challenges are summarized in Table 7.3.

Many of the challenges in Table 7.3 are not unique to USAF; rather, they are shared by any organization seeking to use data science applications such as ML for personnel management and most other business functions. In the following sections, we expand on several of these challenges, which we organize into three broad categories: (1) ethics and privacy, (2) interpretability of ML models, and (3) model performance.

Table 7.3. Challenges of Applying Machine Learning in Organizations

Category	Challenge
Cultural	Data owners may not be incentivized to share data and to meet quality standards
	The organization may lack understanding and skilled personnel for conducting large-scale data science projects
Ethical/legal	Use of data sources alone or together may be restricted
	Prediction composites may exhibit large subgroup differences (i.e., bias)
	Prediction composites may draw on predictor variables with no clear linkage to job in question
	Applicants and recruiters may learn to "game" algorithmic-based decisions
Interpretability	Model predictions may be difficult to explain and anticipate
	Model algorithms may be difficult to explain and justify
Data collection	Data pedigree may be unknown
	Order of precedence for using duplicate variables may be unknown
	Data sets may be small and/or outcomes of interest may be relatively rare
	Data are available only for individuals who meet established criteria for assignment, restricting ranges of input variables
	Historical data do not exist for outcomes in new career fields
Data management	Sources may lack key for mapping linked variables across data sets
	Variable definitions, ranges, and business rules may be undocumented
	Data may lack timestamps
Model stability	Model performance may be sensitive to changes in distributions of input variables
	Model performance may be sensitive to future omission or addition of input variables
	Model performance may become degraded over time in relationship between predictor variables and outcome changes
	Applying model may bias generation of future records used for model training
Model evaluation	Organization may lack agreement and understanding about the outcome(s) to predict and optimize
	Outcome(s) may be difficult to measure, subject to bias, and not entirely dependent on the individual
	Organization may lack a plan and means to track model performance post-deployment
Technical implementation	Models may be prohibitively costly or time-consuming to train
	Model code and data processing pipeline may be error-prone and costly to maintain
	Organization may lack access to standard commercial and open-source tools for data management and ML

SOURCES: Dan J. Putka and Frederick L. Oswald, "Implications of the Big Data Movement for the Advancement of IO Science and Practice," in Scott Tonidandel, Eden B. King, and Jose M. Cortin, eds., *Big Data at Work*, New York: Routledge, 2015; David Sculley, Gary Holt, Daniel Golovin, Eugene Davydov, Todd Phillips, Dietmar Ebner, Vinay Chaudhary, Michael Young, Jean-François Crespo, and Dan Dennison, "Hidden Technical Debt in Machine Learning Systems," in C. Cortes, N. Lawrence, D. Lee, M. Sugiyama, and R. Garnett, eds., *Advances in Neural Information Processing Systems*, Red Hook, N.Y.: Curran Associates, Inc., 2015; and Tonidandel, King, and Cortina, 2018.

Ethics and Privacy

The first set of challenges with ML model use in personnel management decisionmaking relates to ethics and privacy. Title VII of the Civil Rights Act of 1964 prohibits discrimination and protects employees against seemingly neutral practices that may adversely affect protected classes.[9] Variables such as race, gender, and ethnicity may predict first-term and career outcomes yet including them in models may adversely affect people in those classes. Withholding information about an individual's protected statuses may not solve the problem. Other variables strongly associated with protected class status, such as high school or recruiter station location, may produce equivalent effects once demographic variables have been removed from the model. More generally, adopting a data-driven approach may reveal other variables that increase predictive performance yet have no clear relationship with outcomes. Care must be taken when inferring causality and using variables only tenuously linked to outcomes.

Using sources of personally identifiable information raises questions about privacy, especially given the rich and vast scope of data sources potentially available. As a result, the potential for privacy breach when using a data science approach is likely to be greater than for conventional analysis. Due to privacy concerns, there may be restrictions on collecting certain variables that may have predictive power. A related question is who will have access to performance predictions that the ML system produces? Even if predictions are not formally incorporated into personnel management decisions, their disclosure may influence how managers treat individuals.

Interpretability

The power of ML methods is their greater flexibility and thus performance compared with more traditional statistical methods. This comes at the cost of reduced interpretability. Although the significance of individual predictor variables can be demonstrated, as in our analysis in Chapter 4, the cumulation of small contributions from a large number of variables (and the interactions among them) make it hard to anticipate and explain model results. In particular, it is often difficult to explain in a reasonable way why a specific individual received the prediction that he or she did. The lack of transparency associated with these so-called "black-box" approaches is fundamentally at odds with goals for transparency in personnel management systems.

The consequences of reduced interpretability are multifaceted. When an individual is denied a job or opportunity, the complexity of some ML methods and results makes it difficult for an organizational representative (e.g., hiring manager) to explain the decision to that individual as well as to organizational stakeholders (e.g., legal department). ML model interpretability may

---

[9] Although USAF is not subject to this section of law for managing its uniformed (military) personnel, the majority of organizations in the United States (including USAF, as applied to its civilian workforce) must abide by this law. We highlight this to provide context for the ethical challenges that many organizations can face when using ML for human resources (i.e., personnel) management decisionmaking.

also present limits to recruiting in that recruiters will be hard pressed to describe to recruits the set of requirements for entry into different career fields. Finally, the complexity of ML prediction models may obscure implicit biases, raising additional concerns about their ethical use. Before implementing ML methods for decisionmaking, a plan should be established to interpret and explain the impacts on individuals who would be affected (recruits, applicants).

Model Performance

Although our ML models produced moderate to high prediction performance, these results must be considered in light of several limitations, which also apply to traditional statistical models. First, because individuals must meet certain requirements for entry into different USAF specialties, the ranges of input values in historical data are truncated (i.e., values do not exist for those who were not successful in meeting requirements). Outcomes for individuals with values beyond those ranges can be predicted, yet those predictions cannot yet be validated. Second, although the number of records in USAF training databases is large, certain outcomes (i.e., elimination from technical training) are relatively rare, and so the size of the training set is effectively limited. Third, we used historical USAF data (from FY 2004 onward) in our analyses, which may mask important changes in USAF policy and processes (changes to technical training, updates to performance evaluation system, and so on) that affect prediction of future outcomes. In other words, the prediction models have been trained to predict outcomes of the IST and enlisted personnel management systems of yesterday. Finally, the models make no predictions about technical training outcomes for new career fields, for which data do not yet exist.

A final set of considerations pertains to the technical characteristics of the algorithms and their implementations. The more advanced methods we used (i.e., BART) had far greater time complexity than simpler methods. Yet even BART converged within hours, and once trained, all methods essentially return instantaneous predictions for new individuals. We leveraged a wide range of commercial and open-source tools for data preprocessing, model implementation, and model evaluation. To adopt a data science approach, USAF would also need to leverage these resources and build and maintain a data science programming pipeline. These structures require a substantial upfront cost, but once implemented, they would likely not require substantially more effort than current practices.

Concluding Thoughts

We recognize that addressing all of the recommendations will require significant investments. However, there are several things that USAF could do now that require fewer resources, such as retaining data and requiring all recruits to take AF-WIN. To achieve broader objectives to improve job matching, USAF needs to address limitations in existing data and supporting infrastructure. Only then can USAF realize the full potential of contemporary ML tools to increase the quality of classification and reclassification decisions.

Appendix A. Defining and Measuring Success in Personnel Selection

This appendix provides information on the relationships between common predictors and important outcomes from recent quantitative reviews in the personnel selection literature.[1] The summary is not meant to be exhaustive but rather provides context for this report's recommendations regarding additional predictors and outcomes that USAF could systematically measure to improve enlisted classification.

Each quantitative review was organized by the type of predictor and outcome (Table A.1). Specifically, there were seven types of predictors. Five of these predictor sets reflect constructs or individual differences such as general mental ability and personality. The remaining two sets of predictors were specific methods that could be designed to measure a range of individual differences. For example, situational judgment tests could measure leadership, teamwork, or interpersonal skills. The "other" predictor set combines methods such as structured interviews and individual psychological assessments.[2]

We grouped the outcomes into eight categories, with most studies focusing on job performance as typically measured by supervisor ratings. Other outcomes are typically measured using a combination of data from personnel records (e.g., administrative decisions) and self-reported attitudes and behaviors (e.g., satisfaction, commitment, turnover intentions). Some outcomes (e.g., contextual performance, leadership) can also be measured by collecting ratings from peers or other sources familiar with the employee (e.g., subordinates).[3]

We offer a few general observations based on the quantitative reviews summarized in Table A.1. First, personality can predict a wide variety of outcomes including job performance, leadership, and counterproductive work behaviors. Second, interest congruence (i.e., degree of similarity between work-related interests and the job) has emerged as an important predictor of several outcomes, including training and job performance, organizational citizenship behaviors, and turnover. Although these studies provide some indication of recent research, there are many other studies and quantitative reviews that demonstrate relationships between predictors and outcomes. Therefore, we also included several qualitative reviews in the references listed below. In addition to providing more detail about predictors, these qualitative reviews also discuss some predictors not covered in this overview such as integrity and physical ability tests.

---

[1] Articles were identified using the key terms "predictors personnel selection meta" on Google Scholar using a date range of 2010 to current (September 2019).

[2] Individual assessments combine information from multiple sources (e.g., tests, interviews) to guide judgments about a candidate's overall fit for the job/organization.

[3] Walter C. Borman, and Stephan J. Motowidlo, "Task Performance and Contextual Performance: The Meaning for Personnel Selection Research," *Human Performance*, Vol. 10, No. 2, 1997.

Table A.1. Focus of Recent Personnel Selection Quantitative Reviews

Outcome	Description	Predictors						
		General Mental Ability	Specific Aptitudes	Personality—Big-Five Dimensions	Personality—Other Traits	Interests	Situational Judgment Tests	Other
Administrative decisions	Promotions, salary increases, awards							15
Attitudes	Organizational commitment, job satisfaction, turnover intentions				20			
Contextual performance	Organizational citizenship behaviors such as helping, volunteering, taking initiative	9		3		16		
Counter-productive work behaviors	Negative behaviors such as dishonesty, workplace aggression, abusive supervision[a]			1, 8*	17			7
Job performance	Overall job performance, productivity, specific job dimensions (e.g., adaptive performance, oral communication, workplace safety)	13		2, 5, 11, 12, 13, 19	12, 13, 17, 18	16, 20	4	15
Leadership	Leadership effectiveness behaviors such as planning, problem-solving, managing change, and leadership emergence such as promotability			6	6, 10		4	
Training performance	Training success, training progression	21	21			16, 20		21
Withdrawal behaviors	Disengagement from work such as tardiness, absenteeism, and turnover			19		20		

[a] Although academic dishonesty is not a work behavior, we included it because technical training resembles an academic environment. The following sources correspond to the numbers in the predictor categories: (1) Christopher M. Berry, Nichelle C. Carpenter, and Clare L. Barratt, "Do Other-Reports of Counterproductive Work Behavior Provide an Incremental Contribution Over Self-Reports? A Meta-Analytic Comparison," *Journal of Applied Psychology*, Vol. 97, No. 3, 2012; (2) Jeremy M. Beus, Lindsay Y. Dhanani, and Mallory A. McCord, "A Meta-Analysis of Personality and Workplace Safety: Addressing Unanswered Questions," *Journal of Applied Psychology*, Vol. 100, No. 2, 2015; (3) Dan S. Chiaburu, In-Sue Oh, Christopher M. Berry, Ning Li, and Richard G. Gardner, "The Five-Factor Model of Personality Traits and Organizational Citizenship Behaviors: A Meta-Analysis," *Journal of Applied Psychology*, Vol. 96, No. 6, 2011; (4) Michael S. Christian, Bryan D. Edwards, and Jill C. Bradley, "Situational Judgment Tests: Constructs Assessed and a Meta-Analysis of Their Criterion-Related Validities," *Personnel Psychology*, Vol. 63, No. 1, 2010; (5) Brian S. Connelly and Deniz S. Ones, "An Other Perspective on Personality: Meta-Analytic Integration of Observers' Accuracy and Predictive Validity," *Psychological Bulletin*, Vol. 136, No. 6, 2010; (6) Nurcan Ensari, Ronald E. Riggio, Julie Christian, and Gregory Carslaw, "Who Emerges as a Leader? Meta-Analyses of Individual Differences as Predictors of Leadership Emergence," *Personality and Individual Differences*, Vol. 51, No. 4, 2011;(7) Donelson R. Forsyth, George C. Banks, and Michael A. McDaniel, "A Meta-Analysis of the Dark Triad and Work Behavior: A Social Exchange Perspective," *Journal of Applied Psychology*, Vol. 97, No. 3, 2012; (8) Tamara L. Giluk and Bennett E. Postlethwaite, "Big Five Personality and Academic Dishonesty: A Meta-Analytic

Review," *Personality and Individual Differences*, Vol. 72, January 2015; (9) Erik Gonzalez-Mulé, Michael K. Mount, and In-Sue Oh, "A Meta-Analysis of the Relationship Between General Mental Ability and Nontask Performance," *Journal of Applied Psychology*, Vol. 99, No. 6, 2014; (10) Brian J. Hoffman, David J. Woehr, Robyn Maldagen-Youngjohn, and Brian D. Lyons, "Great Man or Great Myth? A Quantitative Review of the Relationship Between Individual Differences and Leader Effectiveness," *Journal of Occupational and Organizational Psychology*, Vol. 84, No. 2, 2011; (11) Jason L. Huang, Ann Marie Ryan, Keith L. Zabel, and Ashley Palmer, "Personality and Adaptive Performance at Work: A Meta-Analytic Investigation," *Journal of Applied Psychology*, Vol. 99, No. 1, 2014; (12) Dana L. Joseph and Daniel A. Newman, "Emotional Intelligence: An Integrative Meta-Analysis and Cascading Model," *Journal of Applied Psychology*, Vol. 95, No. 1, 2010; (13) Dana L. Joseph, Jing Jin, Daniel A. Newman, and Ernest H. O'Boyle, "Why Does Self-Reported Emotional Intelligence Predict Job Performance? A Meta-Analytic Investigation of Mixed EI," *Journal of Applied Psychology*, Vol. 100, No. 2, 2015; (14) Nathan R. Kuncel, Deniz S. Ones, and Paul R. Sackett, "Individual Differences as Predictors of Work, Educational, and Broad Life Outcomes," *Personality and Individual Differences*, Vol. 49, No. 4, 2010; (15) Scott B. Morris, Rebecca L. Daisley, Megan Wheeler, and Peggy Boyer, "A Meta-Analysis of the Relationship Between Individual Assessments and Job Performance," *Journal of Applied Psychology*, Vol. 100, No. 1, 2015; (16) Christopher D. Nye, Rong Su, James Rounds, and Fritz Drasgow, "Interest Congruence and Performance: Revisiting Recent Meta-Analytic Findings," *Journal of Vocational Behavior*, Vol. 98, February 2017; (17) Ernest H. O'Boyle, Jr., Ronald H. Humphrey, Jeffrey M. Pollack, Thomas H. Hawver, and Paul A. Story, "The Relation Between Emotional Intelligence and Job Performance: A Meta-Analysis," *Journal of Organizational Behavior*, Vol. 32, No. 5, 2011; (18) Jonathan A. Shaffer and Bennett E. Postlethwaite, "A Matter of Context: A Meta-Analytic Investigation of the Relative Validity of Contextualized and Noncontextualized Personality Measures," *Personnel Psychology*, Vol. 65, No. 3, 2012; (19) Brian W. Swider and Ryan D. Zimmerman, "Born to Burnout: A Meta-Analytic Path Model of Personality, Job Burnout, and Work Outcomes," *Journal of Vocational Behavior*, Vol. 76, No. 3, 2010; (20) Chad H. Van Iddekinge Philip L. Roth, Dan J. Putka, and Stephen E. Lanivich, "Are You Interested? A Meta-Analysis of Relations Between Vocational Interests and Employee Performance and Turnover," *Journal of Applied Psychology*, Vol. 96, No. 6, 2011; and (21) Matthias Ziegler, Erik Dietl, Erik Danay, Markus Vogel, and Markus Bühner, "Predicting Training Success with General Mental Ability, Specific Ability Tests, and (Un)structured Interviews: A Meta-Analysis with Unique Samples," *International Journal of Selection and Assessment*, Vol. 19, No. 2, 2011.

Appendix B. Descriptive Statistics and Analytic Modeling Results

This appendix provides descriptive statistics for variables used in the analytic models presented in Chapter 4. Additional details and results for the analytic modeling are also provided. In all tables, completeness refers to the percentage of individuals with a value reported for the corresponding variable.

Predictor Characteristics Included in Analytical Models

Table B.1. Demographic Characteristics of Airmen Included in Analytic Models

Variable	Percentage	Completeness (Percentage)
Ethnicity		97
Hispanic/unknown	17.46	
White (non-Hispanic)	82.54	
Gender		98
Female	20.81	
Male	79.19	
Number of dependents		97
0	91.4	
1	5.3	
2 or more	3.3	
Race		97
American Indian/Alaska Native	0.72	
Asian	3.33	
Black/African American	16.48	
Native Hawaiian/other Pacific Islander	1.37	
Two or more races	3.85	
Unknown	0.78	
White	73.48	
First language		100
NA	6.37	
Non-English	8.47	
None	85.16	
Second language		100
NA	6.47	
Non-English	0.87	
None	92.66	

Table B.2. Enlisted Contract Characteristics of Airmen Included in Analytic Models

Variable	Percentage	Completeness (Percentage)
Term of enlistment		100
4	42.17	
6	57.83	
Pay grade		91.7
0–1	69.16	
2	10.26	
3–6	20.58	
Waiver category		6.8
Financial eligibility determination	45.37	
Morals	24.96	
Other	15.53	
Physical standards	14.15	
Waiver status		6.9
Approved	98.73	
Disapproved	1.27	
Bonus category ($)		52.6
0	84.64	
0–5K	8.08	
5K–20K	7.28	

Table B.3. Global Career Clusters Included in Analytic Models

Variable	Percentage	Completeness (Percentage)
AFSC cluster		96.2
Aircraft maintenance	14.26	
Cyber intelligence	5.25	
Facilities	6.4	
Intelligence	7.91	
Material management	8.78	
Medical	7.61	
Other	20.02	
Resource management	7.22	
Space missile management	6.46	
Special operations	16.1	

Table B.4. Initial Preference Variables Included in Analytic Models

Variable	Percentage	Completeness (Percentage)
First AFSC match		93.7
AFSC match	32.2	
MAGE match	12.2	
No match	53.6	
Second AFSC match		50
AFSC match	9.59	
MAGE match	2.14	
No match	88.27	
Third AFSC match		48.7
AFSC match	7.23	
MAGE match	2.37	
No match	90.4	
Fourth AFSC match		47.8
AFSC match	5.7	
MAGE match	7.32	
No match	86.98	

Table B.5. Education and Service Experience Variables Included in Analytic Models

Variable	Percentage	Completeness (Percentage)
Education level		43
College or higher degree	8.71	
High school or less	91.29	
Algebra		94.4
No	3.73	
Yes	96.27	
Biology		94.4
No	7.35	
Yes	92.65	
Chemistry		94.4
No	28.78	
Yes	71.22	
English		94.4
No	2.39	
Yes	97.61	
Geometry		94.4
No	9.61	
Yes	90.39	
Physics		94.4
No	58.49	
Yes	41.51	

Variable	Percentage	Completeness (Percentage)
Trigonometry		94.4
No	66.96	
Yes	33.04	
Typing		94.4
No	26.07	
Yes	73.93	
JROTC		86.4
Completed	4.64	
Didn't participate	84.31	
Other	0.8	
Participated	10.25	
Peace Corps		35.1
No	99.86	
Yes	0.14	

Table B.6. Physical and Medical Variables Included in Analytic Models

Variable	Percentage	Completeness (Percentage)
Strength aptitude test categories		92.5
40–70	5.62	
70	8.63	
80	5.74	
90	6.26	
100	40.41	
110	33.34	
Medical (PULHES ratings)		
Physical		92.5
1	99.87	
2+	0.13	
Upper extremities		92.6
1	99.92	
2+	0.08	
Lower extremities		92.6
1	98.16	
2+	1.84	
Hearing		92.6
1	99.92	
2+	0.08	
Eyes		92.6
1	78.7	
2	21.24	
3+	0.07	
Psychiatric		92.6
1	99.95	
2+	0.05	

Table B.7. Descriptive Statistics for Continuous Variables Included in Analytic Models

Variable	Mean	Standard Deviation	Completeness (Percentage)
Demographics			
Age	20.54	2.27	65.2
Height	68.32	3.44	94.3
Weight	154.44	24.69	94.3
Aptitude			
AFQT score	68.68	16.13	100
MAGE M score	63.45	20.56	100
MAGE A score	70.02	15.45	100
MAGE G score	67.45	17.55	100
MAGE E score	69.82	18.25	100
General science subtest	54.78	7.23	64.7
Arithmetic reasoning subtest	55.47	6.29	94.4
Word knowledge subtest	53.35	6.28	94.4
Paragraph comprehension subtest	55.3	5.62	94.4
Auto-shop information subtests	49.51	8.52	94.4
Math knowledge subtest	57.04	5.57	94.4
Mechanical comprehension subtest	55.3	7.68	94.4
Electrical information subtest	53.79	8.36	94.4
Assembling objects subtest	57.76	6.95	82.6
Personality (TAPAS)			
Achievement	50.03	9.91	37.4
Adjustment	50.23	9.55	37.2
Cooperation	51.84	9.52	35.2
Dominance	50.05	9.78	37.4
Even tempered	52.26	9.38	37.4
Attention-seeking	47.46	9.75	31.2
Selflessness	50.05	9.93	29.1
Intellectual	52.06	9.73	37.4
Nondelinquent	51.57	9.78	37.3
Orderly	49.96	9.75	35.3
Physical conditioning	50.48	9.97	37.4
Self-control	49.79	9.54	35.1
Sociability	48.13	9.97	35.3
Tolerance	52.86	10.17	35.3
Optimism	51.18	9.66	31.3

Table B.8. Descriptive Statistics for Outcome Variables Included in Analytic Models

Variable	Percentage	Completeness (Percentage)
IST outcome		100
Elimination	9.65	
Graduate	77.27	
Washback	13.08	
Promoted to E-5 in first term		38.5
E-5 first term	74.81	
Not E-5 first term	25.19	
Completed first term		67.1
Did not complete first term	70.12	
Completed first term	29.88	
Reenlisted at end of first term		67.1
Did not reenlist	58.28	
Reenlisted	41.72	

Prediction Model Results

The results for all models are summarized here for each of the four outcomes. For each outcome, we present a table with three measures:

- **accuracy:** the number of instances correctly classified divided by the total number of instances
- **AUC:** a measure of how varying the decision threshold affects the trade-off between false positives (i.e., incorrectly predicting that an airman will fail to complete technical training) and true positives (i.e., correctly predicting that an airman will fail to complete technical training), which estimates the probability that a randomly chosen positive example will be rated more highly than a negative example based on the distribution of predicted probabilities
- **confusion matrix:** a tabular display that shows the number of instances by their actual outcomes and their predicted outcomes, with instances falling along the main diagonal reflecting correct classification and instances falling off the main diagonal reflecting incorrect classification.

We visualize the performance for each outcome using ROC plots, with one curve for each model. The diagonal line in the plots represents the predictive performance that comes from simple guessing. Lines that move upward and to the left away from the diagonal imply better predictive performance. AUC is calculated by estimating the actual geometric area under the curve for each model in the square. The diagonal line has AUC 0.5, and a perfect model would have AUC of 1.

Table B.9. Summary of Prediction Performance for Initial Skills Training Graduation

Method	True Value	Confusion Matrix	Predicted Value	Classification Error Percentage	AUC
Baseline model		0	1	7.03	0.761
	0	11,126	20,095		
	1	3,753	304,109		
GLM		0	1	7.07	0.861
	0	11,139	20,082		
	1	3,883	303,981		
Lasso		0	1	7.05	0.860
	0	11,066	20,155		
	1	3,737	304,127		
RFs		0	1	6.97	0.866
	0	1,1521	19,700		
	1	3,918	303,946		
BART		0	1	6.96	0.873
	0	11,496	19,725		
	1	3,890	303,974		

Figure B.1. Receiver Operator Characteristic Curve for Predicted Probabilities of Initial Skills Training Graduation

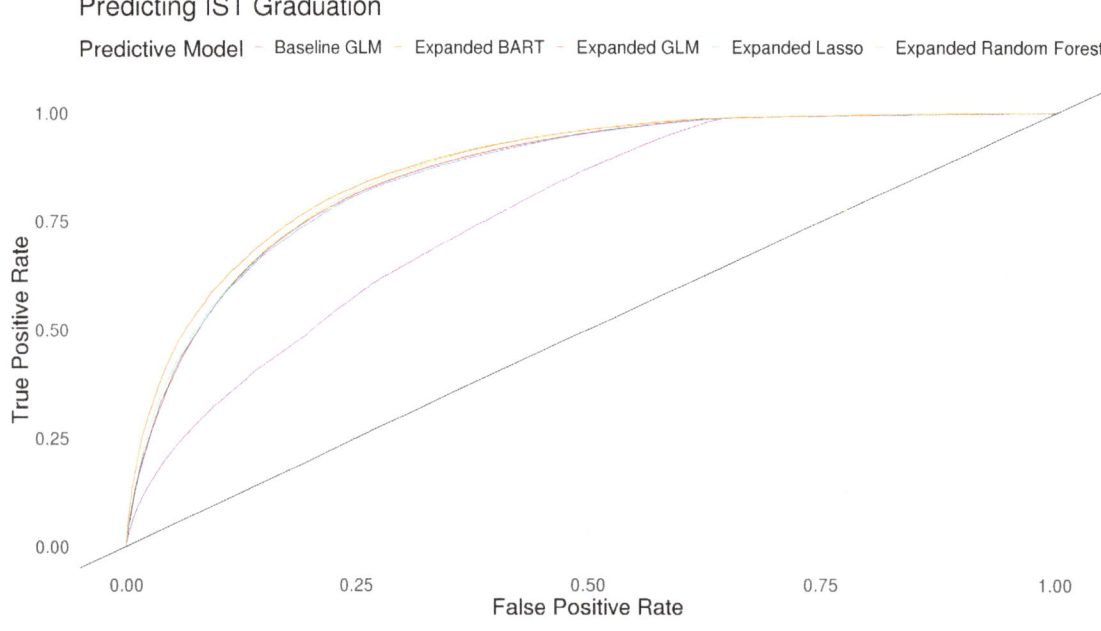

Table B.10. Summary of Prediction Performance for First-Term E-5 Promotion

Method	True Value	Confusion Matrix		Predicted Value	Classification Error Percentage	AUC
Baseline model		0		1	32.36	0.717
	0	118,572		17,041		
	1	48,449		18,322		
GLM		0		1	27.23	0.788
	0	115,901		19,713		
	1	35,388		31,384		
Lasso		0		1	27.36	0.787
	0	116,464		19,150		
	1	36,229		30,543		
RFs		0		1	26.07	0.808
	0	112,990		22,624		
	1	30,146		36,626		
BART		0		1	25.79	0.813
	0	113,148		22,466		
	1	29,730		37,042		

Figure B.2. Receiver Operator Characteristic Curve for Predicted Probabilities of Promotion to E-5 in First Term

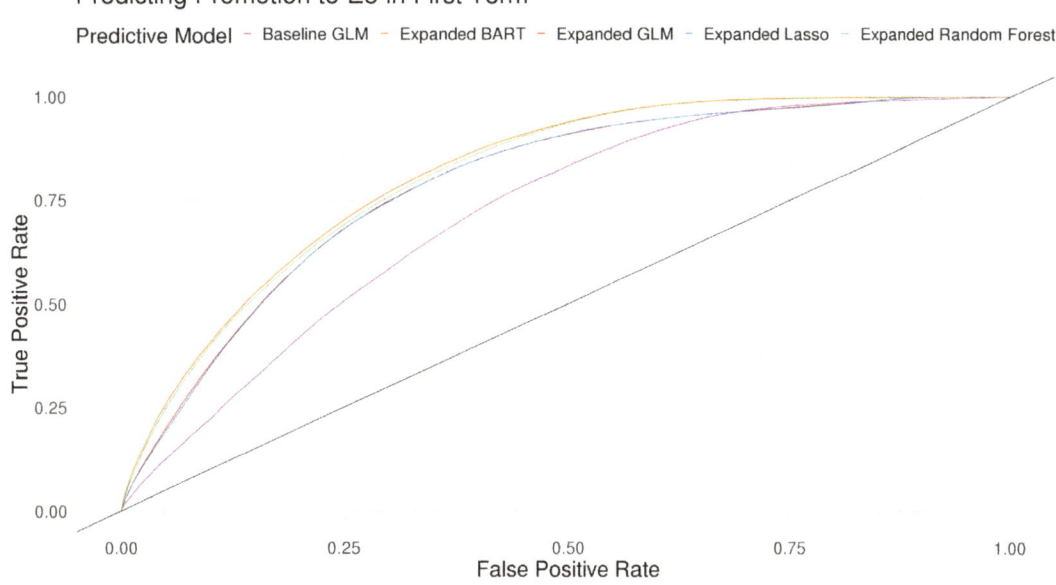

Predicting Promotion to E5 in First Term

Predictive Model — Baseline GLM — Expanded BART — Expanded GLM — Expanded Lasso — Expanded Random Forest

Table B.11. Summary of Prediction Performance for Reenlistment

Method	True Value	Confusion Matrix		Predicted Value	Classification Error Percentage	AUC
		0	1			
Baseline model		0	1		42.26	0.590
	0	86,567	22,991			
	1	61,102	28,347			
GLM		0	1		—	—
	0	—	—			
	1	—	—			
Lasso		0	1		38.57	0.672
	0	73,418	36,140			
	1	40,621	48,830			
RFs		0	1		37.70	0.683
	0	72,052	37,506			
	1	37,529	51,922			
BART		0	1		36.92	0.694
	0	71,100	38,458			
	1	35,018	54,433			

NOTE: GLM did not converge for this model. This can occur when there is separation among outcomes for a given predictor—for example, if everyone who is below age 19 also reenlisted. A GLM model that has many predictors is more likely to run into separation issues.

Figure B.3. Receiver Operator Characteristic Curve for Predicted Probabilities of Reenlistment After First Term

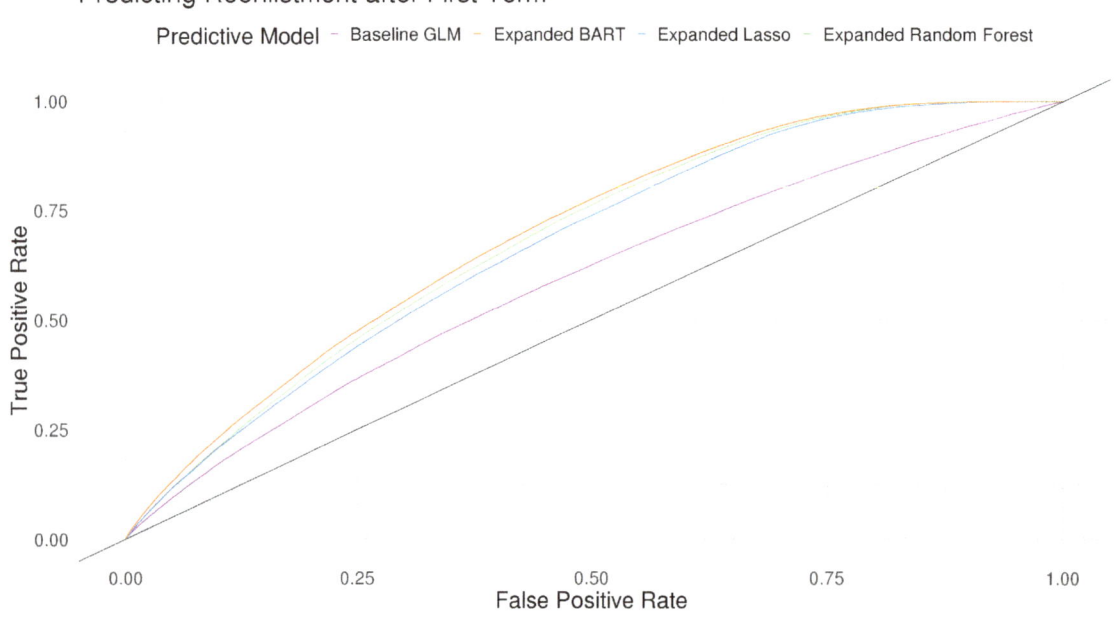

Table B.12. Summary of Prediction Performance for Early Separation

Method	True Value	Confusion Matrix 0	Predicted Value 1	Classification Error Percentage	AUC
Baseline model		0	1	25.35	0.635
	0	147,924	268		
	1	50,188	627		
GLM		0	1	20.78	0.738
	0	143,482	4,712		
	1	36,634	14,181		
Lasso		0	1	20.86	0.737
	0	144,068	4,126		
	1	37,385	13,430		
RFs		0	1	20.20	0.736
	0	143,132	5,062		
	1	35,135	15,680		
BART		0	1	20.08	0.750
	0	142,875	5,319		
	1	34,642	16,173		

Figure B.4. Receiver Operator Characteristic Curve for Predicted Probabilities of Early Separation in First Term

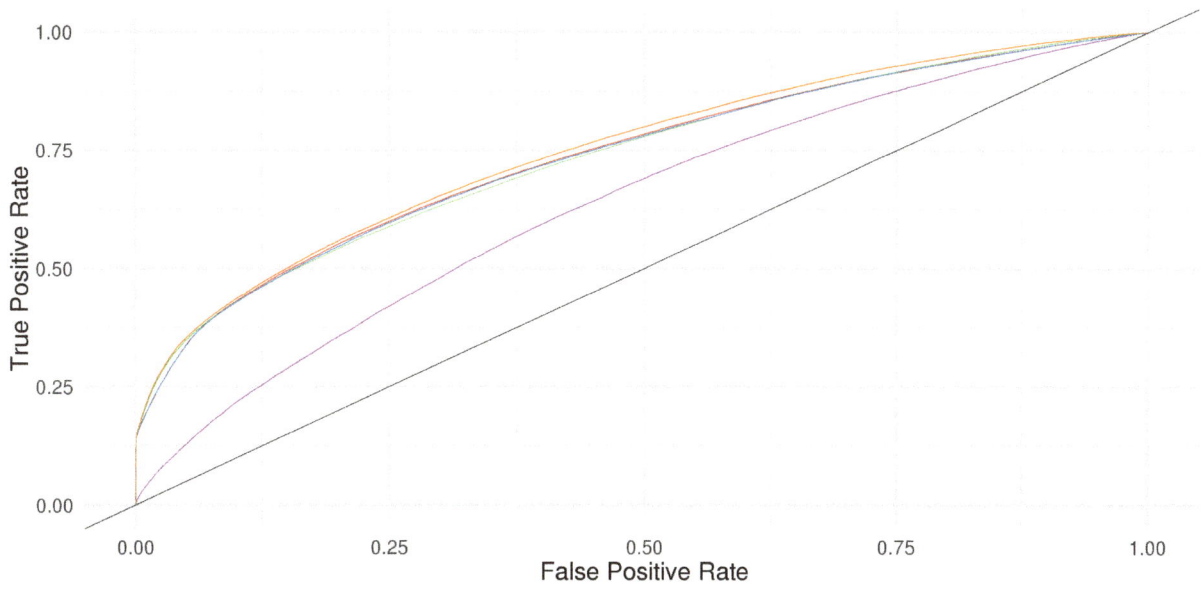

Predicting Early Separation in First Term

Predictive Model — Baseline GLM — Expanded BART — Expanded GLM — Expanded Lasso — Expanded Random Forest

93

Prediction Models Using the Tailored Adaptive Personality Assessment System

Although more TAPAS data are available, only Version 5 has been properly normed for analysis. For this reason, the majority of airmen included in our data set did not have interpretable TAPAS scores. Therefore, we conducted a more limited set of analyses to evaluate the potential contribution of TAPAS in predicting outcomes. We find that including TAPAS improves the performance slightly over the baseline for all four models, but the improvement is smaller than what we saw with the expanded models in the complete analyses.

The results for these models are summarized here for each of the four outcomes. For each outcome, we present a table with the same three measures used to evaluate the more complete models presented above. Please note that because we are working with a very different subset of data, which is not exchangeable with the data used for the complete analyses, the performance results shown here should not be directly compared.

Table B.13. Summary of the Tailored Adaptive Personality Assessment System Prediction Performance for Initial Skills Training Graduation

Method	True Value	Confusion Matrix	Predicted Value	Classification Error Percentage	AUC
Baseline model		0	1	6.37	0.825
	0	816	830		
	1	244	14,973		
TAPAS model		0	1	6.35	0.834
	0	812	834		
	1	237	14,980		

Figure B.5. Receiver Operator Characteristic Curve for the Tailored Adaptive Personality Assessment System Predicted Probabilities of Initial Skills Training Graduation

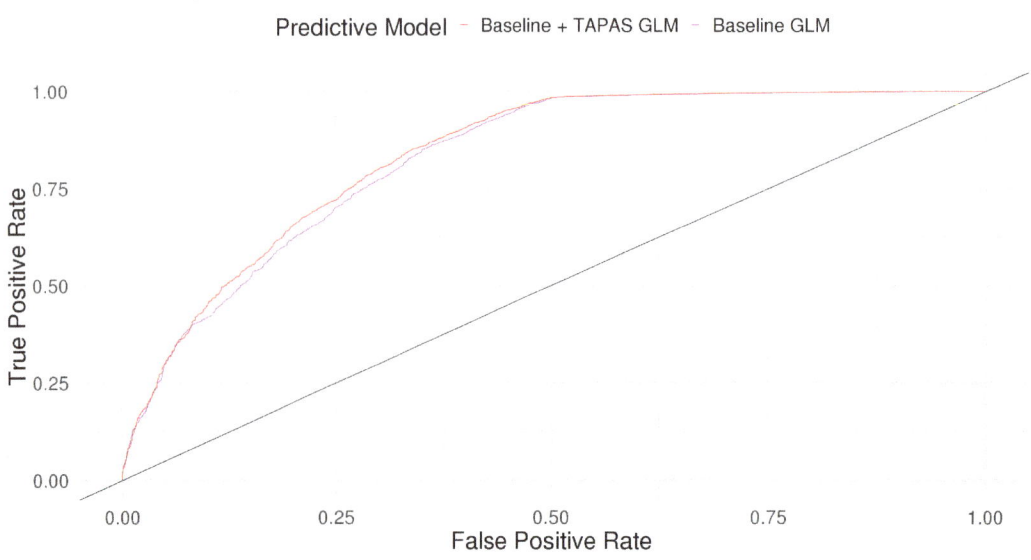

94

Table B.14. Summary of the Tailored Adaptive Personality Assessment System Prediction Performance for Promotion to E-5

Method	True Value	Confusion Matrix	Predicted Value	Classification Error Percentage	AUC
Baseline model		0	1	23.76	0.708
	0	6,233	217		
	1	1,831	337		
TAPAS model		0	1	23.33	0.732
	0	6,201	249		
	1	1,762	406		

Figure B.6. Receiver Operator Characteristic Curve for the Tailored Adaptive Personality Assessment System Predicted Probabilities of Promotion to E-5

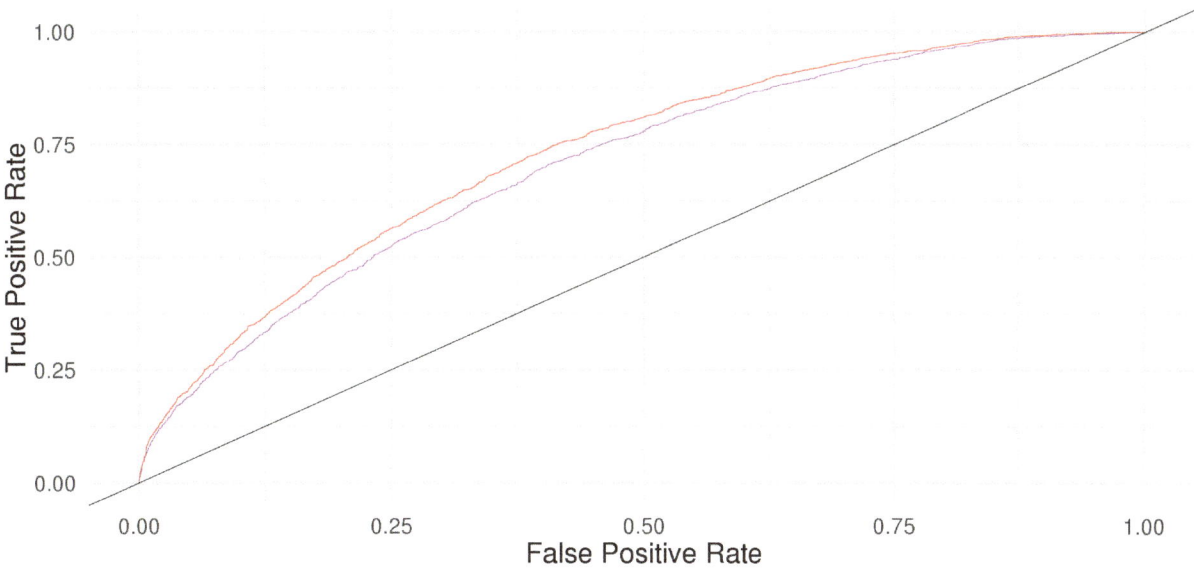

95

Table B.15. Summary of the Tailored Adaptive Personality Assessment System Prediction Performance for Reenlistment

Method	True Value	Confusion Matrix	Predicted Value	Classification Error Percentage	AUC
Baseline model		0	1	36.07	0.699
	0	1,945	1,826		
	1	727	2,579		
TAPAS model		0	1	35.66	0.705
	0	2,028	1,743		
	1	781	2,525		

Figure B.7. Receiver Operator Characteristic Curve for the Tailored Adaptive Personality Assessment System Predicted Probabilities of Reenlistment

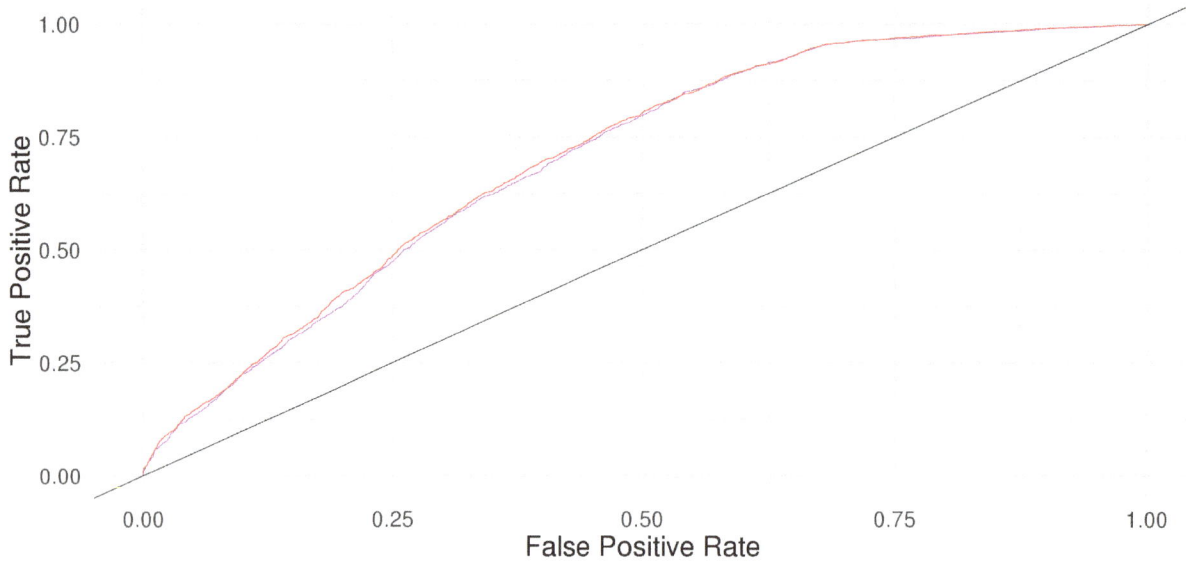

Table B.16. Summary of the Tailored Adaptive Personality Assessment System Prediction Performance for Early Separation

Method	True Value	Confusion Matrix	Predicted Value	Classification Error Percentage	AUC
Baseline model		0	1	15.16	0.629
	0	5,999	0		
	1	1,073	5		
TAPAS model		0	1	15.18	0.653
	0	5,992	7		
	1	1,067	11		

Figure B.8. Receiver Operator Characteristic Curve for the Tailored Adaptive Personality Assessment System Predicted Probabilities of Early Separation

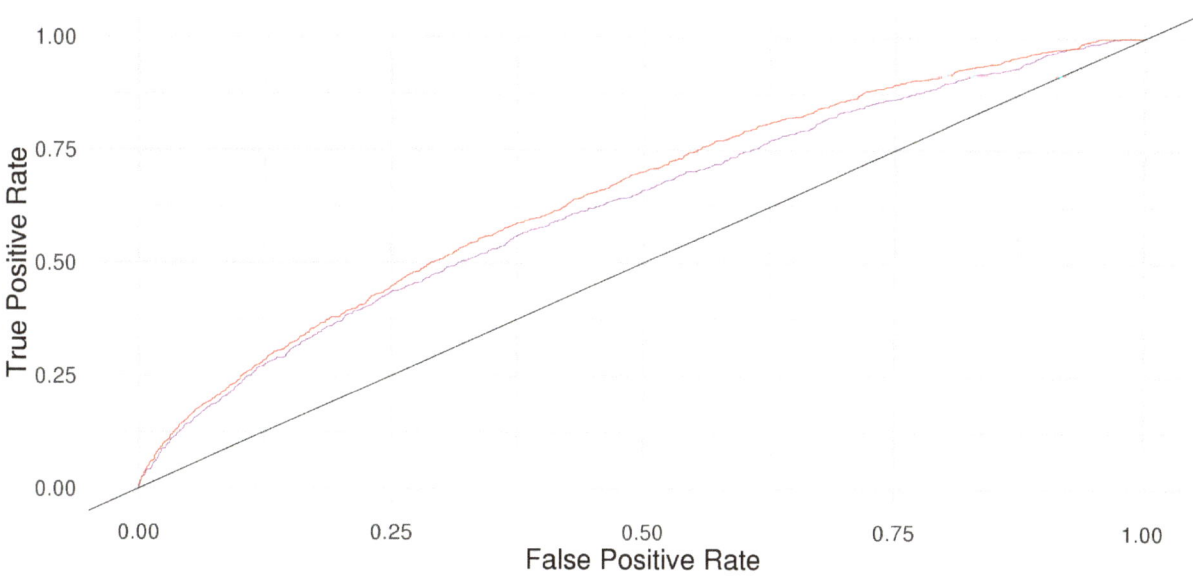

97

Appendix C. Optimization Model Methodology

This appendix provides a detailed mathematical formulation of the optimization model presented in Chapter 5.

Parameters

Let I be the set of airmen needing to be classified and J be the set of AFSCs to which airmen can be assigned to. Then, let c_{ij} be the total cost of reassigning airmen $i \in I$ to AFSC $j \in J$. The cost c_{ij} is determined by two components as follows:

$$(c_{ij} = IDLE_{ij} + RELOCATION_{ij} \ \forall \ i \in I, j \in J,) \tag{1}$$

where $IDLE_{ij}$ is the average cost of having airman i wait for entry into the initial IST course for AFSC j, and $RELOCATION_{ij}$ is the cost of having airman i relocate if assigned to AFSC j.

Optimization with a finite look-ahead period of K weeks (i.e., forcing reclassification of all airmen within K weeks on average) can be enforced by setting the idle costs to $M \gg 0$ if the average frequency of the IST course to enter that AFSC is less than once every K weeks.

Next, we define r_j to be the limit on the number of reclassifications into AFSC $j \in J$ that is estimated from the requirements and priorities in EIS PGL. Moreover, for each airman $i \in I$ to AFSC $j \in J$, let q_{ij} be 1 if the airman previously tried for the given AFSC or is disqualified from it, and 0 otherwise.

Furthermore, we let F be the minimal number of training and career outcomes that are grand successes. Moreover, we define F^{PRO}, F^{REN}, and F^{TRA} to be the minimal number of promotions, reenlistments, and training successes, respectively. Let F^{SEP} be the maximal number of early separations. Let p_{ij} be the probability airmen $i \in I$ will be a grand success if assigned to AFSC $j \in J$ (i.e., complete training, separate early, be promoted, and reenlist). Similarly we define the probabilities of each of the particular training outcomes: p_{ij}^{SEP}, p_{ij}^{PRO}, p_{ij}^{REN}, and p_{ij}^{TRA}.

Decision Variables

Let $x_{ij} \in \{0,1\}$ be the binary decision variables denoting whether airmen $i \in I$ is reclassified to AFSC $j \in J$.

Optimization

Equations (1)–(6) present the optimization model as a binary integer linear program. Equation (1) represents the objective to minimize cost. Constraints (2) enforce that the total assignments to an AFSC are within the requirements. Constraints (3) enforce that exactly 1 AFSC is assigned to each airman. Constraints (4) establish the minimum number of grand successes and the minimum or maximum number of the other outcomes as a result of the reclassifications. Constraints (5) impose that each airman is not assigned to an AFSC that the airman is disqualified for or was previously eliminated from. Constraints (6) impose integrality. An alternative variant of the model that replaces Constraints (4) with a budget constraint and maximizes some training outcome in lieu cost is also possible. The model was programmed in GAMS 24.3.3 and solved using CPLEX 12.6.0.1.

$$\min_{x_{ij}} \sum_{i,j \in I} c_{ij} x_{ij} \tag{1}$$

subject to:

$$\sum_{i \in I} x_{ij} \leq r_j \qquad \forall j \in J \tag{2}$$

$$\sum_{j \in I} x_{ij} = 1 \qquad \forall i \in I \tag{3}$$

$$\sum_{i,j \in I} p_{ij} x_{ij} \geq F \tag{4A}$$

$$\sum_{i,j \in I} p_{ij}^{SEP} x_{ij} \leq F^{SEP} \tag{4B}$$

$$\sum_{i,j \in I} p_{ij}^{PRO} x_{ij} \geq F^{PRO} \tag{4C}$$

$$\sum_{i,j \in I} p_{ij}^{TREN} x_{ij} \geq F^{TREN} \tag{4D}$$

$$\sum_{i,j \in I} p_{ij}^{TRA} x_{ij} \geq F^{TRA} \tag{4E}$$

$$x_{ij} \leq 1 - q_{ij} \qquad \forall i,j \in I \tag{5}$$

$$x_{ij} \in \{0,1\} \qquad \forall i,j \in I. \tag{6}$$

Appendix D. Focus Group Methodology

In this appendix, we provide more detailed information on the focus group methodology, including how we selected specialties and participants to include, how we determined focus group structure, and our qualitative coding analysis steps. We also provide a copy of the focus group protocol and the coding guide.

Approach to Selecting Specialties

To identify specialties to consider for focus groups, we first looked for specialties with above-average numbers and/or percentages of IST reclassifications, based on FY 2017 data (which was available at the time we made the selections), as well as the previous five-year (FY 2002–2017) averages. Although they have among the highest reclassification rates, special warfare specialties were excluded because their selection processes and training pipelines have undergone major changes in recent years, and significant efforts have been made to evaluate challenges with their training attrition.

Our initial selection resulted in the 13 specialties spanning seven career fields, as shown in Table D.1.

Table D.1. Initial List of Specialties and Career Fields Selected for Focus Group Data Collection

Career Field	Specialty Name and Code
CEA	• Aircraft Loadmaster (1A2X1) • Airborne Mission Systems Operator (1A3X1) • Special Missions Aviation (1A9X1)
Command and control systems operations	• ATC (1C1X1)
Cyberspace support	• Cyber Systems Operations (3D0X2) • Client Systems (3D1X1) • Cyber Transport Systems (3D1X2)
Intelligence	• Airborne Cryptologic Language Analyst (1A8X1)[a] • Operations Intelligence (1N0X1) • Cryptologic Language Analyst (1N3X1)
Medical	• Aerospace Medical Service (4N0X1)
Security forces	• Security Forces (3P0X1)
Weather	• Weather (1W0X1)

SOURCE: AFPC, 2018.
[a] This specialty is listed as part of Aircrew Operations (1A) career field but is managed by the career field manager for the intelligence (1N) specialties so we included it with intelligence.

We contacted career field managers and training pipeline staff (e.g., training pipeline managers) for the career fields in Table D.1 to discuss whether the specialties would be good candidates for inclusion in focus groups. Except for one career field, CFMs were available to speak with us and referred us to the appropriate training staff for further discussions.[1] Discussions included consideration of career field training requirements, major changes to the pipelines, and data collection constraints (e.g., whether students would be available in the few months when we could conduct focus groups; whether there would be private rooms to conduct focus groups). Based on these discussions, we selected the nine specialties in Table D.2, which span five occupational categories. Tables D.2 and D.3 provide information about the selected specialties: Table D.2 provides background on job duties and entry requirements whereas Table D.3 provides information on number of students eliminated, graduation rate, and number of students reclassified from each specialty's IST in FY 2018, which is the year of data we used to make decisions about which specialties to include in our focus groups.

Table D.2. Summary of Duties and Entry Requirements for Specialties Included in Focus Groups

Specialty Name and Code	Specialty Summary	MAGE and Entry Test Requirements	Education and Desirable Qualifications
Aerospace Medical Service (4N0X1)	• Plans, provides, and evaluates routine patient care and treatment of beneficiaries to include flying and special operational duty personnel • Organizes, coordinates, executes, and evaluates nursing activities in the medical environment as a Licensed Practical Nurse (LPN)/Licensed Vocational Nurse (LVN) • Performs and directs support activities for patient care situations, including contingency operations and disasters • Performs duty as Flight and Operational Medical Technician (FOMT), Independent Duty Medical Technician (IDMT), Aeromedical Evacuation Technician (AET), Allergy and/or Immunization Technician (AIT), Special Operations Command (SOC) Medic, Critical Care Technician (CCT), National Registry Paramedic (NRP), Neurodiagnostic Technologist (NDT), Dialysis Medical Technician (DMT), or Hyperbaric Medical Technician (HBMT)	• General—50	• Courses in general science, biology, psychology, and chemistry are desirable

---

[1] To protect the identity of the CFMs, we do not divulge who was not available to speak with us.

Specialty Name and Code	Specialty Summary	MAGE and Entry Test Requirements	Education and Desirable Qualifications
Airborne Missions Systems (1A3X1)	• Performs aircrew duties on numerous airborne platforms • Operates, maintains, repairs, and tests airborne communications, electro-optical sensor, radar, computer, EP systems, EW systems • Gathers, records, displays, and distributes mission information. • Interprets computer-generated displays and alarms and Fast Fourier Transform displays • Performs preflight, in-flight, and postflight duties • Supervises and instructs personnel in operation, maintenance, repair, and test procedures • Establishes, manages, and supervises airborne mission system operation and directs aircrew training • Requires, for some missions, nonstandard configurations and penetration into hostile/denied territories undetected utilizing night vision devices and terrain following procedures often in close proximity to other aircraft and operations on unprepared surfaces	• Electronic—70	• Completion of high school is mandatory • Courses in physics, mathematics, and computer principles, typing, speech, and English are desirable
Aircraft Loadmaster (1A2X1)	• Accomplishes preflight and postflight of aircraft and aircraft systems • Receives cargo/passenger load briefings, checks placement of cargo/passengers against aircraft limitations/restrictions, determines adequacy of cargo documentation • If required, services aircraft (i.e., fuel, water, and hydraulics) and creates load plans for cargo and passengers • Supervises cargo/passenger loading and off-loading activities. • Determines cargo placement and restraint requirements and directs and checks the placement of restraint equipment • Computes aircraft weight and balance • Accomplishes passenger comfort activities during flight • Performs aircrew functions and other mission-specific qualification duties to include the airdrop of personnel and equipment/cargo	• General—57	• Completion of high school is mandatory • Courses in mathematics, computer principles, typing, speech, and English are desirable

Specialty Name and Code	Specialty Summary	MAGE and Entry Test Requirements	Education and Desirable Qualifications
Air Traffic Control (1C1X1)	• Controls and regulates en route and terminal air traffic • Initiates and issues ATC clearances, instructions, and advisories to ensure the safe, orderly, and expeditious flow of air traffic operating under instrument and visual flight rules • Plans, organizes, directs, inspects, and evaluates ATC activities	• General—55	• Completion of high school is mandatory • Courses in English are desirable
Client Systems (3D1X1)	• Deploys, sustains, troubleshoots, and repairs standard voice, data, video network, and cryptographic client devices in fixed and deployed environments • Sustains and operates systems through effective troubleshooting, repair, and system performance analysis • Manages client user accounts and organizational client device accounts	1. Electronic—60 OR 2. Electronic 55 and Cyber-Test 60	• Completion of high school or general educational development (GED) equivalency is mandatory • Courses in mathematics, computer science, computer principles, or information technology are desirable • Network or computing commercial certification is desirable
Cyber Systems Operations (3D0X2)	• Installs, supports, and maintains server operating systems or other computer systems and the software applications pertinent to their operation, while also ensuring current defensive mechanisms are in place • Responds to service outages and interruptions to network operations • Administers server-based networked systems, distributed applications, network storage, messaging, and application monitoring required to provision, sustain, operate, and integrate cyber networked systems and applications in garrison and at deployed locations • Has competency in server operating systems, database administration, web technologies, systems-related project management, and supervising cyber systems • Supports identification and remediation of vulnerabilities while enhancing capabilities within cyber environments to achieve desired effects	1. General—64 OR 2. General 54 and Cyber-Test 60	• Completion of high school or GED is mandatory • Courses or certifications in computer and information systems technology are desirable • Network or computing commercial certification is desirable
Cyber Transport Systems (3D1X2)	• Deploys, sustains, troubleshoots, and repairs standard voice, data, and video network infrastructure systems, IP detection systems, and cryptographic equipment • Performs, coordinates, integrates, and supervises network design, configuration, operation, defense, restoration, and improvements	1. Electronic—70 OR 2. Electronic 60 and Cyber-Test 60	• Completion of high school or GED is mandatory • Courses in mathematics, computer science, computer principles, or information technology are desirable • Network or computing commercial certification is desirable

Specialty Name and Code	Specialty Summary	MAGE and Entry Test Requirements	Education and Desirable Qualifications
	• Analyzes capabilities and performance, identifies problems, and takes corrective action • Fabricates, terminates, and interconnects wiring and associated network infrastructure devices		
Security Forces (3P0X1)	• Leads, manages, supervises, and performs security force activities in direct support of two-thirds of the United States Nuclear Enterprise; weapon system and physical security; law and order; military working dog; combat arms and area security operations	• General—30	• Completion of high school or GED is mandatory
Special Missions Aviation (1A9X1)	• Employ fixed-wing, rotary-wing, and tilt-rotor aircraft for special operations, combat rescue, personnel recovery, nuclear security, domestic security, fire-fighting, flight test, and transport for national interest missions that often put them in close proximity to danger, in both time and space • Perform a combination of legacy aviator duties such as that of Flight Engineer, Loadmaster, Aerial Gunner, Navigator, Weapons System Specialist, Electronic Warfare Officer, Radio Operator, Sensor Operator, and Combat Systems Officer. • Perform special mission aviator functions under training and operational conditions • Manage, supervise, train, provide expertise, and evaluate activities • Perform staff functions	• Mechanical—60 and General—57	• Completion of high school or GED is mandatory • Courses in mechanics, mathematics, physics, computer principles, typing, speech, and English are desirable

SOURCE: AFPC, 2018.

Table D.3. Focus Group Training Outcomes, Fiscal Year 2018

Specialty Title	Specialty Code	Number of Eliminations	Graduate Rate	Number of Reclassifications
Aerospace Medical Service	4N0X1	116	0.84	100
ATC	1C1X1	60	0.86	50
Airborne Mission Systems	1A3X1	30	0.89	29
Aircraft Loadmaster	1A2X1	23	0.90	21
Client Systems	3D1X1	61	0.86	56
Cyber Systems Operations	3D0X2	41	0.90	31
Cyber Transport Systems	3D1X2	56	0.87	50
Security Forces	3P0X1	163	0.96	32
Special Missions Aviation	1A9X1	16	0.82	16

NOTE: Estimates based on authors' calculation using USAF personnel data provided to RAND.

Focus Group Participants

We conducted a total of 28 focus groups with 165 airmen currently in IST. Participants were active-duty, NPS airmen who had completed at least several blocks of their IST and were thus able to comment on challenges they may have faced or were facing in completing IST.[2] The exact point in the training pipeline for each AFS was determined in consultation with the training pipeline managers.

In identifying airmen for voluntary participation in the focus groups, RAND researchers worked with local point of contacts for each training pipeline to identify potential participants who were at the designated point of their training and who represented a variety of performance levels in IST to ensure we received various perspectives regarding challenges in IST. We aimed to have a total of four separate focus groups per AFS, with roughly five to seven participants per focus group, but due to logistical reasons we were not able to hold this number of focus groups for each AFS. Table D.4 provides an overview of participant characteristics by AFS. We follow with information about the population of airmen in these specialties, from FY 2018 (see Table D.5).

---

[2] There were seven airmen who participated in the focus groups who were either prior-service or were Air National Guard or Reserve members. Given that they would have different knowledge and experiences with AFS selection, we did not include their comments in that part of the analysis. We did include their comments as part of the analysis exploring experiences within IST.

Table D.4. Focus Group Participant Demographics

	Aerospace Medical (4N0X1)	ATC (1C1X1)	Airborne Mission System (1A3X1)	Loadmaster (1A2X1)	Special Mission Aviation (1A9X1)	Client Systems (3D1X1)	Cyber Systems Operation (3D0X2)	Cyber Transport Systems (3D1X2)	Security Forces (3P0X1)
N	23	23	16	22	9	13	14	28	17
Gender									
Male	12	18	16	19	9	9	12	23	9
Female	11	5	0	3	0	4	2	5	8
Married	7	3	2	4	1	3	1	5	3
Dependents	5	2	1	2	0	1	1	3	0
Education									
GED, or none	0	0	1	1	0	0	0	1	0
High school	9	9	11	9	6	8	8	11	10
Some college	12	7	4	10	3	5	4	13	6
College	2	7	0	2	0	0	2	3	1
Reclassified	2	0	0	0	0	2	0	1	0
Previous service	0	0	0	0	1	0	0	1	0

NOTE: This table includes seven Air National Guard, Reserve, and prior-service participants.

106

Table D.5. Background Characteristics for Fiscal Year 2018 Initial Skills Training Trainees in Specialties Involved in Focus Groups

	Loadmaster (1A2X1)	Airborne Mission System (1A3X1)	Special Mission Aviation (1A9X1)	ATC (1C1X1)	Cyber Systems Operation (3D0X2)	Cyber Transport Systems (3D1X2)	Security Forces (3P0X1)	Aerospace Medical (4N0X1)
N	233	268	89	427	406	421	3,874	711
Gender = M (percentage)	75.1	85.1	91	84.7	82	87.4	70.1	39.8
Marital (percentage)								
Married	7.0	8.2	3.4	13.5	11.2	13.1	7.9	14.8
Single	92.6	90.3	96.6	85.8	88.5	86.2	91.8	84.1
Other	0.4	1.5	0.0	0.7	0.3	0.7	0.3	1.2
Dependents = Yes (percentage)	5.6	9.3	3.4	12.9	10.6	11.2	7.5	13
Reclassified (percentage)	9.0	10.8	18	11.7	7.6	11.9	0.8	14.1
Education (percentage)								
High school or less	5.0	6.9	2.4	3.9	6.5	7.2	3.3	7.5
Some college	80.0	73.1	74.1	75.6	75.1	68.8	85.3	71.8
Graduated college	15.0	20	23.5	20.5	18.4	24	11.4	20.7

Focus Group Structure

Two RAND researchers conducted each focus group in a private classroom at USAF bases where the relevant technical training was located. An experienced senior researcher facilitated the focus group questions, and a second researcher took notes in a manner designed to be as verbatim as possible. Prior to facilitation of the focus groups, all note takers received training on procedures for taking notes to ensure that transcripts were taken in a consistent manner across focus groups. Focus groups began by providing informed consent to all participants, including an overview of the study and the risks and benefits, and noting that all participation was voluntary. Using a semistructured protocol, the focus group questions then focused on three broad areas: (1) the information airmen received on potential careers or specialties when joining USAF and then prior to technical training for their assigned AFS and whether they had received their preferred specialty; (2) experiences in technical training, including perceived factors that contribute to success versus reasons students struggle, washback, or washout; and (3) what preparation airmen had or wish they had to better prepare them for technical training and for suggested changes to training that could help address key challenges or potential barriers to success. The full focus group protocol is included at the end of this appendix. Upon completion of the focus group discussion, we also asked participants to fill out a brief demographic questionnaire. Results from that questionnaire are presented in Table D.4.

Focus Group Analysis

Upon completion of the focus groups, we used special qualitative coding software called NVivo to systematically code the focus group transcripts to identify key themes related to our exploratory questions. In the first phase of our coding, a junior researcher coded all transcripts into broad categories based on the structure of the protocol questions. This coding was conducted under the instruction and supervision of a more experienced senior researcher to ensure that relevant text was being coded appropriately into these categories. Then, in the second phase of our coding, two senior researchers divided up the coding categories to identify more detailed themes. Our analysis also included examining themes by AFS to explore the extent to which the themes we identified were unique to a specific AFS or group of AFSs or were themes common across all AFSs. The full coding guide is provided at the end of this appendix.

It is important to note that in the main body of the report, we do not provide percentages or statistical estimates regarding the prevalence of focus group themes. The goal of these focus groups was exploratory in nature, and given the small number of focus groups per AFS and potential for mixed-responses within a focus group, such percentages could be misleading. In addition, because not every participant responded to each focus group question asked, it was not possible to provide precise statistical estimates regarding the percentage of individuals who made comments associated with a particular theme. Instead, the goal of these focus groups was to gather rich qualitative information on attitudes, knowledge, and experiences that may provide insight into potential improvements for AFS classification and IST.

FOCUS GROUP PROTOCOL

Provide Study Overview and Administer Consent

General Background/Ice Breaker Questions

1. We are first going to begin with questions regarding the characteristics of this group.
    a. When did you join the Air Force?
    b. What phase of training are you currently in?

    [*For question 1b, ask participants if they are all in the same phase of training. If they say that they are, ask which block/course they are in. You do not need to ask this question of each participant in turn if they are in the same phase of training.*]

Career Motivations and Influences

Now, we'd like to ask about your thoughts and experiences when you joined the Air Force and your career preferences.

2. What kind of information did you have on potential careers or specialties you might do in the Air Force when you joined?
    a. Where did you get the information (e.g., recruiter, online, someone you knew in the AF)?
    b. Did the information influence your preferences?
    c. Did you have the opportunity to share your preferences with anyone in an official position (e.g., recruiter) before joining?

3. Did you want to enter the specialty you are now training to enter? Why or why not?
    a. What information do you have on how you were assigned to this specialty?
        i. *Probe if "yes" or positive response*: Is this specialty what you were expecting?
        ii. *Probe if "no" or negative response*: What specialty(ies) were you interested in?
    b. What kind of information did you have about the specialty before entering technical training but after you joined (e.g., while in DEP, BMT)? Did you find the information useful?

We are also interested in hearing about your thoughts and experiences in technical training.

4. What factors do you think contribute to success in training for this specialty?

   a. *Probe:* How do factors such as student characteristics, relationships that students have with others, and aspects of training contribute to success in this pipeline?
   Examples if needed:

      i. Student characteristics: knowledge, skills, or abilities (for example: aptitude); personality, morals, attitudes

      ii. Relationships with others (for example: peers, instructors, other staff)

      iii. Training aspects: course content, course difficulty, length

5. What do you think is the most typical reason that that students struggle, washback, or washout from this training pipeline?

   a. *Probe:* What are the most challenging aspects of training for this specialty?

6. What preparation did you have (or wish you had) to be successful in this training pipeline?

   a. *Probe:* Do you have experiences that helped to prepare you (example: high school courses, hobbies)?

   b. *Probe*: Is there anything you wish you had known or had done to better prepare for training?

7. What can be changed about training to help students succeed?

Closing Questions

8. What do you think is the most important factor in student success in this training pipeline?

9. Is there anything important for us to know about training for this specialty that we haven't asked you about or any key takeaways we should have for how the Air Force could help better support students in completing BMT and training for this specialty?

BACKGROUND INFORMATION

1. What is your current rank?

   _____

2. Have you previously served in the military?

   o Yes
   o No

3. Which component of the Air Force are you a part of?

   o Active Duty Air Force
   o Air National Guard
   o Air Force Reserves

4. When did you complete BMT?

   o Month _____
   o Year _____

5. What specialty are you training to enter?

   _____

6. Have you been reclassified from one AFSC to another?

   o Yes
   o No
   o Not sure

7. What is the highest level of education you have completed?

   o GED, or no high school degree
   o High school
   o Some college
   o College graduate
   o Graduate school degree (e.g., law degree, master's degree, M.D., Ph.D.)

8. What is your marital status?

   o Single (never married)
   o Married
   o Divorced or separated
   o Widowed

9. Do you have children?

- o Yes
- o No

10. What is your gender?

- o Female
- o Male
- o Do not wish to answer

Coding Guide

Background Codes: To capture the background of the focus groups, first code all text by focus group AFS.

Content Codes: Once all focus group notes are coded by AFS, code the discussion text for content and themes. Code all text that addresses the code (i.e., theme) as defined below. Although corresponding protocol questions are provided for reference, code text on each theme throughout the transcripts, not just in response to the corresponding protocol question. Level 1 codes are the broadest, with subsequent codes becoming increasingly specific with each level. Code at the most specific level possible. Code as many content codes as are relevant to the text, such that multiple codes may be applied to the same text.

See Table D.6 for the coding scheme used for the focus groups.

Table D.6. Content Coding Scheme for Focus Groups

Level 1	Level 2	Level 3	Level 4	Description	Corresponding Protocol Question
Career motivations and influences	Info on USAF careers and AFSs				What kind of information did you have on potential careers or specialties you might do in the Air Force when you joined?
		Knowledgeable?			What kind of information did you have on potential careers or specialties you might do in the Air Force when you joined?
			Yes	Comments about having relevant information on USAF careers or specialties	
			No or limited	Comments about having limited or no relevant information on USAF careers or specialties	
		Source			Where did you get the information (e.g., recruiter, online, someone you knew in the AF)?
			AF website	Comments about using the official USAF website as a source of information	
			Family	Comments about family being a source of information	
			Friends	Comments about friends being a source of information	
			Internet/ social media	Comments about using the internet or social media as a source of information; any official USAF website should NOT be included here, but should be in the USAF website code	
			Recruiter	Comments about a recruiter being a source of information	
			Other	Other sources that do not fit under other codes	

114

Level 1	Level 2	Level 3	Level 4	Description	Corresponding Protocol Question
		Influence on preferences		Comments about whether the degree to which information airmen obtained influenced their preferences	Did the information influence your preferences?
		Opportunity to share preferences			Did you have the opportunity to share your preferences with anyone in an official position (e.g., recruiter) before joining?
			Yes	Comments about having an opportunity to share preferences (e.g., dream sheet)	
			No/ guided or constrained	Comments about not having an opportunity to share preferences or feeling like they were guided or constrained to put only certain preferences (e.g., recruiter instructed them to write down certain jobs or put a certain job at the top of their list)	
	AFS interest				Did you want to enter the specialty you are now training to enter? Why or why not?
			Yes	Comments about wanting to enter the specialty; note that this would include comments about the specialty being somewhere on their list, even if not at the top	
			No	Comments about NOT wanting to enter the specialty	
	AFS assignment info			Comments regarding what they knew or did not know about how they were assigned their specialty	What information do you have on how you were assigned to this specialty?
		Requirements		Descriptions that include the importance of requirements for getting an assignment (e.g., ASVAB, physical requirements)	
		Needs of USAF		References to the "needs of USAF" or recruiters needing to find airmen for certain jobs as influencing assignments	
		None or limited		Comments that they had none or limited information on why they were assigned their specialty	

Level 1	Level 2	Level 3	Level 4	Description	Corresponding Protocol Question
	AFS info prior to IST				What kind of information did you have about the specialty before entering technical training but after you joined (e.g., while in DEP, BMT)? Did you find the information useful?
		Knowledgeable?			
			Yes	Comments about having relevant information before entering technical training	
			No or limited	Comments about having limited or no relevant information before entering technical training	
		Source			
			AF website	Comments about using the official USAF website as a source of information	
			Family	Comments about family being a source of information	
			Friends	Comments about friends being a source of information	
			Internet/ social media	Comments about using the internet or social media as a source of information; any official USAF website should NOT be included here, but should be included in the USAF website code	
			Recruiter	Comments about a recruiter being a source of information	
			BMT	Comments about information in BMT as a source of information (e.g., MTIs, specialty book)	
			Other	Other sources that do not fit under other codes	
		Preferred specialties		Discussion of which specialty they preferred instead of their current specialty	What specialty(ies) were you interested in?
		IST expectations			Is this specialty what you were expecting?
			Different	Discussions of ways in which IST was different from what they expected	
			Same	Discussions of ways in which IST was similar to what they expected	

Level 1	Level 2	Level 3	Level 4	Description	Corresponding Protocol Question
IST experiences					
	Factors for success				What factors do you think contribute to success in training for this specialty?
		Student characteristics		Comments about individual's characteristics or attributes that contribute to success in IST	
		Relationships with others		Comments about student's relationships with others (e.g., peers, instructors) that contribute to success in IST	
		Training aspects		Comments about aspects of technical training that support success in IST	
			Instructor knowledge or approach	Comments about instructors' knowledge of IST subject matter or teaching approach or methods that contribute to IST success	
		Environment-related		Comments about the environment outside of the classroom that contribute to success in IST	
		Other		Other factors for success not captured by existing codes	
		Most important factor			What do you think is the most important factor in student success in this training pipeline?
			Drive	Comments about student's' drive or motivation being the most important factor to success in IST	
			Studying	Comments about time committed to studying being the most important factor to success in IST	
			Other	Other most important factors not captured by existing codes	
	Reasons for struggle, washout, or other challenges				What do you think is the most typical reason that that students struggle, washback, or washout from this training pipeline?
		Environment-related		Comments about the environment outside of the classroom that contribute to challenges in IST	

117

Level 1	Level 2	Level 3	Level 4	Description	Corresponding Protocol Question
		Student characteristics		Comments about individual's characteristics or attributes that contribute to challenges in IST	
		Difficulties with training requirements or content		Comments about student's difficulties with IST requirements or training content that contribute to challenges in IST	
		Resources or instructor related		Comments about training resources (e.g., simulators, textbooks) or instructors that contribute to challenges in IST	
		Other		Other challenges or reasons for washback or washout not captured by existing codes	
	Helpful preparation				What preparation did you have (or wish you had) to be successful in this training pipeline?
		What DID help			Do you have experiences that helped to prepare you (e.g., high school courses, hobbies)?
			Prior education	Comments describing student's prior education or training that helped prepare for IST	
			Relevant experience	Comments describing student's relevant experience prior to training that helped prepare for IST	
			Other	Other comments about experiences that helped students prepare for IST not captured by existing codes	
		What WOULD HAVE helped			Is there anything you wish you had known or had done to better prepare for training?
			Better info on training content or requirements	Comments related to receiving more information about IST content or requirements that would have helped student better prepare for training	

Level 1	Level 2	Level 3	Level 4	Description	Corresponding Protocol Question
			Info about environment	Comments related to receiving more information about the environment during IST that would have helped student better prepare for training	
			Physical prep (work out)	Comments related to student preparing better physically prior to training to help with IST preparation	
			Specific education or training	Comments about specific education or training that would have helped student better prepare for IST	
			Other	Other comments regarding what would have helped student better prepare for IST that are not captured by existing codes	
		Nothing did or could help		Comments that nothing helped student prepare or could have helped student prepare for IST	
	Changes to training				What can be changed about training to help students succeed?
		Timing or more time		Comments regarding IST changes related to timing of training	
		Out of class environment		Comments regarding IST changes related to the environment outside the classroom	
		Resources, instructors, teaching methods		Comments regarding IST changes related to training resources, instructors, or teaching methods	
		Course content changes		Comments regarding IST changes to the course content	
		Better info about AFS or training		Comments regarding changes related to providing better information about an AFS or IST prior to training	
		Other		Other comments about changes to IST not captured by existing codes	
Miscellaneous comments				Comments that are important but do not fit into one of the current codes	
For discussion				Comments that need to be discussed by research team (e.g., which code to use)	

119

References

Aerospace Medical Service Apprentice (AMSA) Curriculum Plan, Fort Sam Houston, Tex.: Medical Education and Training Campus, October 29, 2018.

AFPC—*See* U.S. Air Force Personnel Center.

Alley, William E., Leticia J. Pachecho, David B. Birkelbach, Kenneth L. Schwartz, and Johnny J. Weissmuller, *Modeling Individual Performance Criteria in the Air Force*, AFCAPS-FR-2010-0015, San Antonio, Tex.: Operational Technologies Corp., 2007.

Bai, Lu, Rob Meredith, and Frada Burstein, "A Data Quality Framework, Method and Tools for Managing Data Quality in a Health Care Setting: An Action Case Study," *Journal of Decision Systems*, Vol. 27, No. 1, April 16, 2018, pp. 144–154.

Berry, Christopher M., Nichelle C. Carpenter, and Clare L. Barratt, "Do Other-Reports of Counterproductive Work Behavior Provide an Incremental Contribution over Self-Reports? A Meta-Analytic Comparison," *Journal of Applied Psychology*, Vol. 97, No. 3, 2012, pp. 613–636.

Berry, Christopher M., Melissa L. Gruys, and Paul R. Sackett, "Educational Attainment as a Proxy for Cognitive Ability in Selection: Effects on Levels of Cognitive Ability and Adverse Impact," *Journal of Applied Psychology*, Vol. 91, No. 3, 2006, pp. 696–705.

Beus, Jeremy M., Lindsay Y. Dhanani, and Mallory A. McCord, "A Meta-Analysis of Personality and Workplace Safety: Addressing Unanswered Questions," *Journal of Applied Psychology*, Vol. 100, No. 2, 2015, pp. 481–498.

Borman, Walter C., and Stephan J. Motowidlo, "Task Performance and Contextual Performance: The Meaning for Personnel Selection Research," *Human Performance*, Vol. 10, No. 2, 1997, pp. 99–109.

Breiman, Leo, "Statistical Modeling: The Two Cultures," *Statistical Science*, Vol. 16, No. 3, 2001, pp. 99–231.

Campion, Michael A., "Meaning and Measurement of Turnover: Comparison of Alternative Measures and Recommendations for Research," *Journal of Applied Psychology*, Vol. 76, No. 2, 1991, pp. 199–212.

Cappelli, Peter, Prasanna Tambe, and Valery Yakubovich, "Artificial Intelligence in Human Resources Management: Challenges and a Path Forward," Social Science Research Network, 2018. As of January 22, 2019:
https://papers.ssrn.com/sol3/papers.cfm?abstract_id=3263878

Carretta, Thomas R., "Predictive Validity of the Armed Services Vocational Aptitude Battery for Several US Air Force Enlisted Training Specialties," Air Force Research Laboratory/Human Effectiveness Directorate, Dayton, Ohio: Wright-Patterson Air Force Base, 2014.

Cawley, John, and Johanna Catherine Maclean, "Unfit for Service: The Implications of Rising Obesity for US Military Recruitment," *Health Economics*, Vol. 21, No. 11, 2012, pp. 1348–1366.

Chalfin, Aaron, Oren Danieli, Andrew Hillis, Zubin Jelveh, Michael Luca, Jens Ludwig, and Sendhil Mullainathan, "Productivity and Selection of Human Capital with Machine Learning," *American Economic Review*, Vol. 106, No. 5, 2016, pp. 124–127.

Chiaburu, Dan S., In-Sue Oh, Christopher M. Berry, Ning Li, and Richard G. Gardner, "The Five-Factor Model of Personality Traits and Organizational Citizenship Behaviors: A Meta-Analysis," *Journal of Applied Psychology*, Vol. 96, No. 6, 2011, pp. 1140–1166.

Chien, Chen-Fu, and Li-Fei Chen. "Data Mining to Improve Personnel Selection and Enhance Human Capital: A Case Study in High-Technology Industry," *Expert Systems with Applications*, Vol. 34, No.1, 2008, pp. 280–290.

Christian, Michael S., Bryan D. Edwards, and Jill C. Bradley, "Situational Judgment Tests: Constructs Assessed and a Meta-Analysis of Their Criterion-Related Validities," *Personnel Psychology*, Vol. 63, No. 1, 2010, pp. 83–117.

Cohen, Jacob, "A Power Primer," *Psychological Bulletin*, Vol. 112, No. 1, 1992, pp. 155–159.

Connelly, Brian S., and Deniz S. Ones, "An Other Perspective on Personality: Meta-Analytic Integration of Observers' Accuracy and Predictive Validity," *Psychological Bulletin*, Vol. 136, No. 6, 2010, pp. 1092–1122.

Corbin, Juliet M., and Anselm L. Strauss, *Basics of Qualitative Research: Techniques and Procedures for Developing Grounded Theory*, 3rd ed., Thousand Oaks, Calif.: Sage Publications, 2008.

Dalal, Reeshad S., "A Meta-Analysis of the Relationship Between Organizational Citizenship Behavior and Counterproductive Work Behavior," *Journal of Applied Psychology*, Vol. 90, No. 6, 2005, pp. 1241–1255.

Department of Defense Manual 5210.42, *Nuclear Weapons Personnel Reliability Program*, Washington, D.C.: U.S. Department of Defense, 2018.

Earles, James A., and Malcolm James Ree, "The Predictive Validity of the ASVAB for Training Grades," *Educational and Psychological Measurement*, Vol. 52, No. 3, 1992, pp. 721–725.

Ensari, Nurcan, Ronald E. Riggio, Julie Christian, and Gregory Carslaw, "Who Emerges as a Leader? Meta-Analyses of Individual Differences as Predictors of Leadership Emergence," *Personality and Individual Differences*, Vol. 51, No. 4, 2011, pp. 532–536.

Forsyth, Donelson R., George C. Banks, and Michael A. McDaniel, "A Meta-Analysis of the Dark Triad and Work Behavior: A Social Exchange Perspective," *Journal of Applied Psychology*, Vol. 97, No. 3, 2012, pp. 557–579.

Fox, Suzy, Paul E. Spector, and Don Miles, "Counterproductive Work Behavior (CWB) in Response to Job Stressors and Organizational Justice: Some Mediator and Moderator Tests for Autonomy and Emotions," *Journal of Vocational Behavior*, Vol. 59, No. 3, 2001, pp. 291–309.

Garb, Howard N., James M. Wood, Kristin Schneider, Monty Baker, and Wendy Travis, "Suitability Screening During Basic Military Training," *Military Psychology*, Vol. 25, No. 1, 2013, pp. 82–91.

Geman, Stuart, Elie Bienenstock, and René Doursat, "Neural Networks and the Bias/Variance Dilemma," *Neural Computation*, Vol. 4, No. 1, 1992, pp. 1–58.

Giluk, Tamara L., and Bennett E. Postlethwaite, "Big Five Personality and Academic Dishonesty: A Meta-Analytic Review," *Personality and Individual Differences*, Vol. 72, January 2015, pp. 59–67.

Gonzalez-Mulé, Erik, Michael K. Mount, and In-Sue Oh, "A Meta-Analysis of the Relationship Between General Mental Ability and Nontask Performance," *Journal of Applied Psychology*, Vol. 99, No. 6, 2014, pp. 1222–1243.

Google, "Machine Learning," webpage, January 22, 2019. As of September 16, 2019:
https://developers.google.com/machine-learning/glossary/#m

Gudivada, Venkat, Amy Apon, and Junhua Ding, "Data Quality Considerations for Big Data and Machine Learning: Going Beyond Data Cleaning and Transformations," *International Journal on Advances in Software*, Vol. 10, No. 1, 2017, pp. 1–20.

Harold, Crystal M., Lynn A. McFarland, and Jeff A. Weekley, "The Validity of Verifiable and Non-Verifiable Biodata Items: An Examination Across Applicants and Incumbents," *International Journal of Selection and Assessment*, Vol. 14, No. 4, 2006, pp. 336–346.

Harrington, Lisa M., Kathleen Reedy, John A. Ausink, Bart E. Bennett, Barbara Bicksler, Darrell D. Jones, and Daniel Ibarra, *Air Force Non-Rated Technical Training: Opportunities for Improving Pipeline Processes*, Santa Monica, Calif.: RAND Corporation, RR-2116-AF, 2017. As of July 20, 2020:
https://www.rand.org/pubs/research_reports/RR2116.html

Hastie, Trevor, Robert Tibshirani, and Jerome Friedman, *The Elements of Statistical Learning: Data Mining, Inference and Prediction*, New York: Springer, 2015.

Hoffman, Brian J., David J. Woehr, Robyn Maldagen-Youngjohn, and Brian D. Lyons, "Great Man or Great Myth? A Quantitative Review of the Relationship Between Individual Differences and Leader Effectiveness," *Journal of Occupational and Organizational Psychology*, Vol. 84, No. 2, 2011, pp. 347–381.

Hooper, Amy C., Cheryl Paullin, Dan J. Putka, and William S. Strickland, *An Empirical Analysis of Reasons for Attrition Among First-Term Airmen in the United States Air Force*, Alexandria, Va.: Human Resources Research Organization, 2008.

Huang, Jason L., Ann Marie Ryan, Keith L. Zabel, and Ashley Palmer, "Personality and Adaptive Performance at Work: A Meta-Analytic Investigation," *Journal of Applied Psychology*, Vol. 99, No. 1, 2014, pp. 162–179.

Johnson, James F., Sophie Romay, and Laura Barron, "Air Force Work Interest Navigator (AF-WIN) to Improve Person-Job Match: Development, Validation, and Initial Implementation," *Military Psychology*, Vol. 32, No. 1, 2019, pp. 111–126.

Joseph, Dana L., Jing Jin, Daniel A. Newman, and Ernest H. O'Boyle, "Why Does Self-Reported Emotional Intelligence Predict Job Performance? A Meta-Analytic Investigation of Mixed EI," *Journal of Applied Psychology*, Vol. 100, No. 2, 2015, pp. 298–342.

Joseph, Dana L., and Daniel A. Newman, "Emotional Intelligence: An Integrative Meta-Analysis and Cascading Model," *Journal of Applied Psychology*, Vol. 95, No. 1, 2010, pp. 54–78.

Kuncel, Nathan R., Deniz S. Ones, and Paul R. Sackett, "Individual Differences as Predictors of Work, Educational, and Broad Life Outcomes," *Personality and Individual Differences*, Vol. 49, No. 4, 2010, pp. 331–336.

Manacapilli, Thomas, Carl F. Matthies, Louis W. Miller, Paul Howe, P. J. Perez, Chaitra M. Hardison, H. G. Massey, Jerald Greenberg, Christopher Beighley, and Carra S. Sims, *Reducing Attrition in Selected Air Force Training Pipelines*, Santa Monica, Calif.: RAND Corporation, TR-955-AF, 2012. As of December 10, 2019: https://www.rand.org/pubs/technical_reports/TR955.html

Markham, Ina S., "Assessing the Prediction of Employee Productivity: A Comparison of OLS vs. CART," *International Journal of Productivity and Quality Management*, Vol. 8, No. 3, 2011, pp. 313–332.

McCloy, R. S., Rodney A. McCloy, Michael Ingerick, and William J. Strickland, *Towards an Advanced Personnel Accessioning System*, Alexandria, Va.: HumRRO, FR 08-40, 2008.

Morris, Scott B., Rebecca L. Daisley, Megan Wheeler, and Peggy Boyer, "A Meta-Analysis of the Relationship Between Individual Assessments and Job Performance," *Journal of Applied Psychology*, Vol. 100, No. 1, 2015, pp. 5–20.

Mount, Michael K., Lisa A. Witt, and Murray R. Barrick, "Incremental Validity of Empirically Keyed Biodata Scales over GMA and the Five Factor Personality Constructs," *Personnel Psychology*, Vol. 53, No. 2, 2000, pp. 299–323.

Nye, Christopher D., Rong Su, James Rounds, and Fritz Drasgow, "Interest Congruence and Performance: Revisiting Recent Meta-Analytic Findings," *Journal of Vocational Behavior*, Vol. 98, February 2017, pp. 138–151.

O'Boyle, Ernest H., Jr., Ronald H. Humphrey, Jeffrey M. Pollack, Thomas H. Hawver, and Paul A. Story, "The Relation Between Emotional Intelligence and Job Performance: A Meta-Analysis," *Journal of Organizational Behavior*, Vol. 32, No. 5, 2011, pp. 788–818.

Putka, Dan J., Adam S. Beatty, and Matthew C. Reeder, "Modern Prediction Methods: New Perspectives on a Common Problem," *Organizational Research Methods*, Vol. 21, No. 3, 2018, pp. 689–732.

Putka, Dan J., and Frederick L. Oswald. "Implications of the Big Data Movement for the Advancement of IO Science and Practice," in Scott Tonidandel, Eden B. King, and Jose M. Cortin, eds., *Big Data at Work*, New York: Routledge, 2015, pp. 195–226.

Rose, Mark R., Gregory G. Manley, and Johnny J. Weissmuller. *Development of Two-And Three-Factor Classification Models for Air Force Battlefield Airmen (BA) and Related AFSs*, San Antonio, Tex.: Air Force Personnel Center, Randolph Air Force Base, No. AFCAPS-TR-2013-0007, 2013.

Rumsey, Michael G., and Jane M. Arabian, "Military Enlistment Selection and Classification: Moving Forward," *Military Psychology*, Vol. 26, No. 3, 2014, pp. 221–251.

Sculley, David, Gary Holt, Daniel Golovin, Eugene Davydov, Todd Phillips, Dietmar Ebner, Vinay Chaudhary, Michael Young, Jean-François Crespo, and Dan Dennison, "Hidden Technical Debt in Machine Learning Systems," in C. Cortes, N. Lawrence, D. Lee, M. Sugiyama, and R. Garnett, eds., *Advances in Neural Information Processing Systems*, Red Hook, N.Y.: Curran Associates, Inc., 2015, pp. 2503–2511.

Shaffer, Jonathan A., and Bennett E. Postlethwaite, "A Matter of Context: A Meta-Analytic Investigation of the Relative Validity of Contextualized and Noncontextualized Personality Measures," *Personnel Psychology*, Vol. 65, No. 3, 2012, pp. 445–494.

Skinner, Jacobina, Nancy Thompson, Kenneth Schwartz, and Johnny Weissmuller, *Air Force Personnel Research Issues: A Manager's Handbook*, San Antonio, Tex.: Operational Technologies Corp., 2007.

Snow, Richard E., and David F. Lohman, "Toward a Theory of Cognitive Aptitude for Learning from Instruction," *Journal of Educational Psychology*, Vol. 76, No. 3, 1984, pp. 347–376.

Sparkman, Bryan, *Technical Training Job Spin User's Manual*, USAF-AETC, San Antonio, Tex.: Randolph Air Force Base, 2010.

Stark, Stephen, Oleksandr S. Chernyshenko, Fritz Drasgow, Christopher D. Nye, Leonard A. White, Tonia Heffner, and William L. Farmer, "From ABLE to TAPAS: A New Generation of Personality Tests to Support Military Selection and Classification Decisions," *Military Psychology*, Vol. 26, No. 3, 2014, pp. 153–164.

Strohmeier, Stefan, and Franca Piazza, "Domain Driven Data Mining in Human Resource Management: A Review of Current Research," *Expert Systems with Applications*, Vol. 40, No. 7, 2013, pp. 2410–2420.

Swider, Brian W., and Ryan D. Zimmerman, "Born to Burnout: A Meta-Analytic Path Model of Personality, Job Burnout, and Work Outcomes," *Journal of Vocational Behavior*, Vol. 76, No. 3, 2010, pp. 487–506.

Tonidandel, Scott, Eden B. King, and Jose M. Cortina, "Big Data Methods: Leveraging Modern Data Analytic Techniques to Build Organizational Science," *Organizational Research Methods*, Vol. 21, No. 3, 2018, pp. 525–547.

U.S. Air Education and Training Command Instruction 36-2605, "Formal Flying Training Administration and Management," San Antonio, Tex.: Randolph Air Force Base, 2017.

USAF—*See* U.S. Air Force

U.S. Air Force, "Aerospace Medical Service," webpage, undated a. As of September 13, 2019: https://www.airforce.com/careers/detail/aerospace-medical-service

———, "Airborne Mission Systems Specialist," webpage, undated b. As of September 13, 2019: https://www.airforce.com/careers/detail/airborne-mission-systems-specialist

———, "Air Traffic Control," webpage, undated c. As of September 13, 2019: https://www.airforce.com/careers/detail/air-traffic-control

———, "Client Systems," webpage, undated d. As of September 13, 2019: https://www.airforce.com/careers/detail/client-systems

———, "Cyber Systems Operations," webpage, undated e. As of May 24, 2021: https://www.airforce.com/careers/detail/cyber-systems-operations

———, "Cyber Transport Systems," webpage, undated f. As of September 13, 2019: https://www.airforce.com/careers/detail/cyber-transport-systems

———, "Frequently Asked Questions: Where Can I Take the ASVAB?" webpage, undated g. As of September 15, 2019: https://www.airforce.com/frequently-asked-questions/enlisted-path/where-can-i-take-the-asvab

————, "Meet Requirements," webpage, undated h. As of August 22, 2019:
https://www.airforce.com/how-to-join/prepare-for-success/meet-requirements

————, "Security Forces," webpage, undated i. As of September 13, 2019:
https://www.airforce.com/careers/detail/security-forces

————, "Technical Training," webpage, undated j. As of September 16, 2019:
https://www.airforce.com/education/technical-training

U.S. Air Force Instruction 48-123, *Medical Examinations and Standards*, November 5, 2013.

U.S. Air Force Manual 36-2100, *Military Utilization and Classification*, April 7, 2021. As of
May 25, 2021:
https://static.e-publishing.af.mil/production/1/af_a1/publication/afman36-2100/afman36
-2100.pdf

U.S. Air Force Manual 36-2647, *Institutional Competency Management and Development*,
March 25, 2014. As of April 21, 2021:
https://www.ang.af.mil/Portals/77/documents/force_dev/AFD-150528-002.pdf?ver=2016-09
-21-092900-540

U.S. Air Force Personnel Center, *Air Force Enlisted Classification Directory (AFECD): The
Official Guide to the Air Force Enlisted Classification Codes*, Randolph, Tex.: Air Force
Public Affairs Agency, April 30, 2018.

U.S. Air Force Recruiting Service Instruction 36-2001, "Recruiting Procedures for the Air
Force," 2012.

U.S. Code, Title 10, Chapter 31, "Enlistments," September 8, 1980. As of January 27, 2021:
https://www.law.cornell.edu/uscode/text/10/subtitle-A/part-II/chapter-31

U.S. General Services Administration, "Privately Owned Vehicle (POV) Mileage
Reimbursement Rates," webpage, September 13, 2019. As of September 14, 2019:
https://www.gsa.gov/travel/plan-book/transportation-airfare-rates-pov-rates/privately-owned
-vehicle-pov-mileage-reimbursement-rates

Van Iddekinge, Chad H., Philip L. Roth, Dan J. Putka, and Stephen E. Lanivich, "Are You
Interested? A Meta-Analysis of Relations Between Vocational Interests and Employee
Performance and Turnover," *Journal of Applied Psychology*, Vol. 96, No. 6, 2011,
pp. 1167–1194.

Ziegler, Matthias, Erik Dietl, Erik Danay, Markus Vogel, and Markus Bühner, "Predicting
Training Success with General Mental Ability, Specific Ability Tests, and (Un)structured
Interviews: A Meta-Analysis with Unique Samples," *International Journal of Selection and
Assessment*, Vol. 19, No. 2, 2011, pp. 170–182.

Lightning Source UK Ltd.
Milton Keynes UK
UKHW051110310522
403750UK00005B/66

9 781977 407023